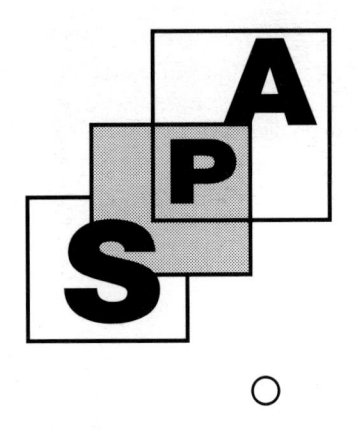

SPA
Steps in Phonics Assessment

Teacher's Pack

Deborah Oldham

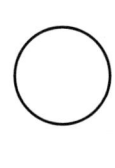

Hodder & Stoughton
A MEMBER OF THE HODDER HEADLINE GROUP

A non-photocopiable **Individual Record Sheet** to track pupil progress is available separately to accompany this **Teacher's Pack**, and is designed to provide a continuous record from school admission through to mastery of Step 7. The **Individual Record Sheet** is packaged in sets of 20 copies (ISBN 0 340 79948 X)

For convenience and clarity throughout this Teacher's Pack, the child is referred to throughout as *he* and the teacher as *she* (or *you*).

Orders: please contact Bookpoint Ltd, 39 Milton Park, Abingdon, Oxon OX14 4TD. Telephone: (44) 01235 400414, Fax: (44) 01235 400454. Lines are open from 9.00 – 6.00, Monday to Saturday, with a 24-hour message answering service. Email address: orders@bookpoint.co.uk

British Library Cataloguing in Publication Data
A catalogue record for this title is available from The British Library

ISBN 0 340 79947 1
First published 2000
Impression number 10 9 8 7 6 5 4 3 2 1
Year   2005 2004 2003 2002 2001 2000

Copyright © 2000 Deborah Oldham

All rights reserved. This work is copyright. Permission is given for copies to be made of pages specifically identified as being photocopiable, provided they are used exclusively within the institution for which this work has been purchased. For reproduction for any other purpose, permission must first be obtained in writing from the publishers.

Printed in Great Britain for Hodder & Stoughton Educational, a division of Hodder Headline Plc, 338 Euston Road, London NW1 3BH, by Hobbs The Printers, Totton, Hants.

Contents

INTRODUCTION 5

USING STEPS IN PHONICS ASSESSMENT 9
Classroom use of the assessments
Whole-school use of the assessments

INTERPRETING THE STEP SCORES 15

STEP ONE 16
The Step 1 assessments

STEP TWO 17
Rationale
Administration
Testing the child
Scoring the Step 2 tests

STEP THREE 20
Rationale
Administration
Testing the child
Scoring the Step 3 tests

STEP FOUR 25
Rationale
Administration
Testing the child
Scoring the Step 4 tests

STEP FIVE 32
Rationale
Administration
Testing the child
Scoring the Step 5 tests

STEP SIX 38
Rationale
Administration
Testing the child
Scoring the Step 6 tests

STEP SEVEN 41
Rationale
Administration
Testing the child
Scoring the Step 7 tests

PHOTOCOPIABLE ASSESSMENT RESOURCES 44

Introduction

This series of assessments has been devised to test children's acquisition and use of phonic skills. The reading assessments do not attempt to test reading comprehension skills.

The assessments are primarily intended for use with Reception and Key Stage One pupils, but practice has shown that children acquire phonic skills, like many other skills, at different rates. Therefore these assessments can also be used with older children or those with special educational needs.

Those assessments at **Steps 4–7** which involve reading and spelling words in the context of sentences have been designed to be as simple as possible and to relate to the experiences of young school children. The aim is also for children to see reading and spelling in the context of wider communication skills.

The assessments use as reference, and are keyed to:

- the Early Learning Goals for Language and Literacy;
- the National Literacy Strategy, in particular List 3 from the Appendices: Summary of the specific phonics and spelling work to be covered in Years R to 2;
- the DFEE publication *Progression in Phonics* and accompanying CD-ROM (March 2000).

Steps in Phonics Assessment follows the 'steps' recommended in *Progression in Phonics* for the teaching and learning of phonics. Each of the seven **Steps** comprises a number of constituent skills which are assessed separately, as follows:

Step 1 [Nursery/Reception]

The child has:
- skills of hearing and discriminating general sounds, speech sounds and patterns.

Step 2 [Reception]

The child can:
A. Orally continue a rhyming string.
B. Hear the initial phonemes: **s m c/k t g h.**
C. Say the initial phonemes: **s m c/k t g h.**
D. Recognise the initial graphemes: **s m c/k t g h.**
E. Write the initial graphemes: **s m c/k t g h.**

Step 3   **[Reception/Year 1]**

The child can:
- A. Hear the final phonemes: **s m c/k t g**.
- B. Say the final phonemes: **s m k t g**.
- C. Recognise the final graphemes: **s (ss) m ck t g**.
- D. Write the final graphemes: **s (ss) m ck t g**.
- E. Hear the initial phonemes: **l n d sh ch**.
- F. Say the initial phonemes: **l n d sh ch**.
- G. Recognise the initial graphemes: **l n d k sh ch**.
- H. Write the initial graphemes: **l n d k sh ch**.
- I. Hear the final phonemes: **l (ll) n d sh ch**.
- J. Say the final phonemes: **l (ll) n d sh ch**.
- K. Recognise the final graphemes: **l (ll) n d sh ch**.
- L. Write the final graphemes: **l (ll) n d sh ch**.

Step 4   **[Reception/Year 1]**

The child can:
- A. Hear the medial vowel phonemes: **a e i o u**.
- B. Say the medial vowel phonemes: **a e i o u**.
- C. Recognise the medial vowel graphemes: **a e i o u**.
- D. Write the medial graphemes: **a e i o u**.
- E. Hear the initial phonemes: **f qu b r j p th**.
- F. Say the initial phonemes: **f qu b r j p th**.
- G. Recognise the initial graphemes: **f qu b r j p th**.
- H. Write the initial graphemes: **f qu b r j p th**.
- I. Hear the final phonemes: **f (ff) b p th ng**.
- J. Say the final phonemes: **f (ff) b p th ng**.
- K. Recognise the final graphemes: **f (ff) b p th ng**.
- L. Write the final graphemes: **f (ff) b p th ng**.
- M. Spell Consonant-Vowel-Consonant words.
- N. Read Consonant-Vowel-Consonant words.

Step 5   **[Reception/Year 1]**

The child can:
- A. Hear the initial/final phonemes: **v w y z x**.
- B. Say the initial/final phonemes: **v w y z x**.
- C. Recognise the initial/final graphemes: **v w y z x**.
- D. Write the initial/final graphemes: **v w y z x**.
- E. Hear the phonemes within initial consonant clusters: **bl br cl cr dr dw fl fr gl gr pl pr sc scr sk sl sm sn sp spl spr squ st str sw tr tw thr shr**
- F. Say the phonemes within initial consonant clusters: **bl br cl cr dr fl fr gl gr pl pr sc scr sk sl sm sn sp squ st sw tr tw thr**
- G. Hear the phonemes within final consonant clusters: **ld nd lk nk sk lp mp sp ct ft lt nt pt st xt lf nch lth**
- H. Say the phonemes within final consonant clusters: **ld nd lk nk sk lt nt st lf nch**

I. Spell words built from initial Consonant clusters plus Vowel plus Consonant
J. Read words built from initial Consonant clusters plus Vowel plus Consonant
K. Spell words built from Consonant plus Vowel plus Consonant cluster
L. Read words built from Consonant plus Vowel plus Consonant cluster

Step 6 [Year 1/Year 2]

The child can:

A. Spell words with common long vowel digraphs (Consonant plus long-Vowel grapheme plus Consonant) using most common rimes:
   ai – aid ail ain
   ee – eed eek eel eep eet
   ie – ie ied
   oa – oad oal oap oat
   oo – oof ool oom oon oot

B. Read words with common long vowel digraphs (Consonant plus long-Vowel grapheme plus Consonant) using most common rimes:
   ai – aid ail ain
   ee – eed eek eel eep eet
   ie – ie ied
   oa – oad oal oap oat
   oo – oof ool oom oon oot

C. Spell words with more common vowel digraphs (Consonant plus Vowel grapheme plus Consonant) using most common rimes:
   or – ork orn ort
   ar – ard ark arm arn arp art
   ir – ird irl irt
   oi – oil oin
   ou – out

D. Read words with more common vowel digraphs (Consonant plus Vowel grapheme plus Consonant) using most common rimes:
   or – ork orn ort
   ar – ard ark arm arn arp art
   ir – ird irl irt
   oi – oil oin
   ou – out

Step 7 [Year 1/Year 2]

The child can:

A. Spell words built from more long-vowel digraphs and trigraphs, using most common patterns:

long **a** – ay ace ade age ake ale ame ape ave
long **e** – ead eaf eal eam ean eap eat
long **i** – igh ight -y ice ide ife ike ile ime ine ipe ive
long **o** – ode oke ole ome one ope ose ote -oe ow
long **u** – ew ue ude une use ute

B. Read words built from more long-vowel digraphs and trigraphs, using most common patterns:

long **a** – ay ace ade age ake ale ame ape ave
long **e** – ead eaf eal eam ean eap eat
long **i** – igh ight -y ice ide ife ike ile ime ine ipe ive
long **o** – ode oke ole ome one ope ose ote -oe ow
long **u** – ew ue ude une use ute

C. Spell words built from more common vowel digraphs and trigraphs, using most common patterns:

oy – oy
ow (ou) – owl own
ow (oa) – ow own
er – erd erm
ur – url urt
aw – awk awl
air – air
ear – ear (fear)
oo – ood ook

D. Read words built from more common vowel digraphs and trigraphs, using most common patterns:

oy – oy
ow (ou) – owl own
ow (oa) – ow own
er – erd erm
ur – url urt
aw – awk awl
air – air
ear – ear (fear)
oo – ood ook

Using Steps in Phonics Assessment

CLASSROOM USE OF THE ASSESSMENTS

Assessment of individual children

At **Steps 1 to 4**, the single letters – plus **qu, sh, ch, ck, th,** and **ng** – are taught in groups of five to seven phonemes, and they are assessed in these same groups. Similarly, the style of assessment reflects the teaching approach, which should take the form of aural and oral activities, accompanied by the recognition of the appropriate graphic symbol, and the opportunities to learn to write the grapheme correctly. (The less-used **v, w, x, y** and **z** are introduced at the start of **Step 5**.)

The last parts of the **Step 4** tests assess the child's ability to use his knowledge of phonemes and graphemes to read and spell words. Having reached this point in the development of his phonic skills, the child is ready to begin blending consonants for reading and spelling, continually building upon the skills he has learnt.

The child will progress to learning to read and spell vowel digraphs and trigraphs. He will then have the skills to read and spell hundreds of words, and the phonological awareness to recognise patterns and rhymes, the ability to learn rules and irregularities, and the confidence to further extend his language development.

Each assessment can be administered after a Step has been taught, to check:
- if the objectives have been achieved, and therefore gauge the success of the teaching activities;
- if the time-scale for teaching each Step is appropriate;
- if a child is experiencing difficulties with any particular aspects of the phonics work.

Because each Step assessment is divided into Parts, it is very easy to diagnose any problems, and to provide further or specific activities to address the child's difficulties. Look for patterns of errors, as recorded on the Teacher Recording Sheet, to make full diagnostic use of the assessment information available at each Step.

- **Problems with hearing and saying sounds, or visual discrimination, or poor fine motor skills,** may have a physical cause which can be medically investigated and advice sought.

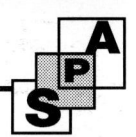

These problems may be solved by providing more activities and games which require the child to:
- complete an alliterative pattern;
- create rhyming strings;
- identify and match phonemes in initial, medial and final positions.

- **Problems with phoneme-grapheme correspondence** will need to be addressed by a variety of activities and games which encourage the child to:
  - relate a phoneme to its written form by listening to sounds in words and writing the required grapheme;
  - relate a grapheme to its spoken form: *'What sound is this?'*

- **Problems segmenting words for spelling** can be addressed by providing activities and games which break words down into their phonemes. Spelling real words is an important stage in the development of phonic skills, and should follow on naturally from previous classroom phonic experiences.

- **Problems blending words for reading** can be addressed by providing activities and games which require the child to recognise the graphic representations of sounds. For example, a child who tries to read the word 'train' as 't-r-a-i-n' (five phonemes) has not yet learnt the graphic representation 'ai' as a 'long a' sound.

Examples of games and activities to address these problems can be found in *Progression in Phonics*, and in many other published materials.

By using the appropriate test after each Step has been taught, teaching and learning objectives can be modified and adapted. This is particularly useful for those children with special educational needs who have a 'phonics' target on their Individual Education Plan.

An **Individual Record Sheet** is available separately to accompany **Steps in Phonics Assessment,** and is designed to provide a continuous record of individual pupil progress from school admission through to mastery of **Step 7**.

The front page is an 'at-a-glance' summary of the child's progress in the development of his phonic skills during his first years at school. It is also a useful way to gauge the speed of his progress.

The subsequent pages form a record of the child's progress in achieving the objectives for each of the separate phonics skills which comprises each Step. It can thus be a very useful diagnostic tool as well as a measure of progress, and a useful basis for establishing realistic individual targets.

General administration of the assessments

Step 1 comprises a series of informal assessments, which are recorded on to a photocopiable Teacher Recording Sheet.

Steps 2, 3, 4 and 5 consist of parts where the child is asked to:
- listen and respond orally;
- look at pictures and respond orally;
- listen and respond by pointing;

as well as parts where he has to:
- look at pictures and write;
- spell words to dictation;
- listen to words, read and select them from choices by circling.

Where possible, the 'stimulus' pictures or words are provided as reusable **Resource Sheets**, which can be photocopied on to card (perhaps using a different colour for each Step) and laminated. The teacher records the child's oral and pointing responses using the photocopiable **Teacher Recording Sheets** provided (on which the target words are substituted for pictures).

At **Steps 4, 5, 6 and 7**, the children are asked to complete photocopiable **Test Sheets.**

For those children who take longer than others to achieve a Step, it is very important to have a written record of their responses in order to be able to diagnose any problems; and to gauge their progress.

Those parts where the children have to write themselves form the written record. Once the children are consistently secure at each of the Steps, the teacher can decide if the test sheets need to be retained.

The **Individual Record Sheet** will track each child's progress.

WHOLE-SCHOOL USE OF THE ASSESSMENTS

Target-setting

It is possible to use the assessments in conjunction with the *Progression in Phonics* teaching programme to set targets. Every school is advised to set targets for literacy, and many have chosen to specify phonics as an area for development.

To set effective targets, there needs to be a start date and a finish date.

Most schools will assess their children in June – towards the end of the school year. If the target period is to be a year (June to June), then the June starting data can be compared to the June finishing data. (The June finishing data then becomes the starting data for the next target cycle.)

For each class teacher, the target-setting period is likely to be September to June, so the individual teacher can measure the success of her own teaching, and the children's learning, whilst the children are in her class.

At each assessment point, the children should be entered at the Step at which the teacher considers they will succeed. It is not necessary, or advisable, to start at **Step 1** each time the tests are used (unless a child has specific problems and progress is to measured by an improvement within the test).

Effective target-setting involves both an analysis of data and the use of the teacher's professional knowledge and judgement.

A target-setting example

A class of 28 mixed ability Year 1 children

In June of their Reception Year the children were tested by their class teacher, and a **class record sheet** (see page 13) completed, listing the results of all individual children. This showed that in this class:
- 6 children had achieved the objectives of **Step 4**;
- 18 children had achieved the objectives of **Step 3**;
- 4 children had achieved the objectives of **Step 2**.

In the first few weeks of the children's Autumn Term in Year 1, the teacher gathers a considerable amount of information about each child, and – with the information passed on from the Reception teacher – makes a judgement on which Step the child will achieve in June. Individual children's targets

Steps in Phonics Assessment — Class Record Sheet

Year : 1 Teacher : Mrs Wood		Interim assessments at any appropriate times - mid-year, after Step completed, etc.			Set in September of Y1	
Child's name	Start date : June YR	Date :	Date :	Date :	Target	Finish date : June Y1
Amy	4	5		6	**7**	7
Beth	4	5		6	**7**	7
Callum	4	5		6	**7**	7
Darren	4	5	6		**7**	7
Emma	4	5		6	**7**	7
Fran	4	5		6	**7**	7
Gwyn	3		5	6	**6**	7
Harry	3		4	5	**6**	6
Ian	3	4	5		**6**	6
James	3		4	5	**6**	6
Keri	3		4	5	**6**	6
Lucy	3		4	5	**6**	6
Michael	3		4	5	**6**	6
Nicola	3	4	5		**6**	6
Olena	3	4		5	**6**	6
Peter	3		4	5	**6**	6
Philip	3	4	5		**6**	6
Rachel	3	4	5		**6**	6
Ryan	3	4		5	**6**	6
Stephen	3		4	5	**6**	6
Susi	3		4	5	**6**	6
Terry	3	4		5	**6**	6
Tracey	3		4	5	**6**	6
Una	3	4	5		**6**	6
Vicki	2		3		**4**	4
Wanda	2			3	**4**	4
Will	2			3	**4**	4
Yvonne	2		3		**4**	4

are formally recorded. The class record sheet shows as targets that:
- some children (6) will have achieved the objectives of **Step 7**;
- most children (18) will have achieved the objectives for **Step 6**;
- some children (4) will have achieved the objectives for **Step 4**.

In June at the end of Year 1 the children are assessed by their class teacher. From her knowledge of each child's progress made during the school year, and the possible use of the tests after each Step, the Year 1 teacher decides which tests it is appropriate for each child to attempt (see Interpreting the Step Scores, opposite). The data can then be compared, and the success of the targets evaluated.

Outcomes will:
- give a basis for evaluating the success of the teaching;
- suggest possible amendments to the *present* teacher's planning, in terms of...
  - grouping children according to their learning needs;
  - using specific phonic activities within the Literacy Hour;
  - the use of additional support and resources;
  - the *Progression in Phonics* teaching time-scales;
  - the teaching programme for children with special educational needs;
- influence the future planning of the *next* year's teacher.

Interpreting the Step Scores

The **Steps in Phonics Assessment** tests are designed to assess 'criterion mastery' – the extent to which a child has achieved the specified skills at each Step – rather than to give age-related, normative scores which do not directly inform teaching.

Each scoring table, for **Steps 2–7**, has two columns (see, for example, page 19).

The left-hand column shows the range of scores between 50% and 80%.
- *Any child who is likely to score less than 50% should not take the test*, as he has not yet developed the necessary phonic skills.
- A child who scores between 50% and 80% is well on his way to achieving the objectives for that Step.

An analysis of the scores for the various Parts of each Step will show in which areas the child needs more practice:

Possible problems may lie in:
- identifying rhymes;
- hearing phonemes;
- saying phonemes;
- recognising graphemes;
- writing graphemes;
- segmenting words for spelling;
- blending words for reading.

Appropriate phonic activities can then be planned and any continuing learning or physical difficulties addressed.

The right-hand column shows the range of scores between 80% and 100%.

A score within this range is what most children should achieve, assuming they have not been tested prematurely, and indicates that the child is ready to progress to the next Step.

STEP ONE

> During their time in Nursery and/or Reception, children will be working towards the **Early Learning Goals**. There are several areas of the *Early Learning Goals* for Language and Literacy which set objectives for the end of the Foundation Stage and are intrinsic to **Step 1**:
>
> 'Most children will be able to:
> - enjoy listening to and using spoken language, and readily turn to it in their play and learning;
> - explore and experiment with sounds;
> - listen with enjoyment and respond to stories, songs and other music, rhymes and poems;
> - extend their vocabulary, exploring the sounds of new words.'

Step 1 is a preparation stage for later, more formal phonics teaching.

Children need to have experienced many activities like those suggested in *Progression in Phonics*, and to have achieved a degree of skill in them, in order to progress onto further Steps. These activities, and the development of the children's skills, form an important part of good early years practice.

THE STEP 1 ASSESSMENTS

Teacher Recording Sheet 1 is designed for on-going informal assessment, although it is possible to arrange a set time to work towards most of the children achieving the objectives of **Step 1**. Some of the information can be recorded following Baseline Assessment of the children on entering Reception. Other information can be recorded from informal assessment of the children's response to normal classroom activities.

The children must be able to:
- recognise sounds in the environmental generally, and different 'instrumental' sounds;
- discriminate speech sounds in voice games.

They should also be given opportunities to:
- experience rhythm and rhyme, and join in with rhyming games;
- join in with alliterative games.

Early identification of problems is vital at this stage. From the **Step 1** assessments, all future phonics teaching can be planned. *It is necessary for the children to have the skills developed in* **Step 1** *before starting* **Step 2**.

STEP TWO

> **National Literacy Strategy** – Reception
> **Early Learning Goals:**
> ■ 'hear and say initial ... sounds in words;
> ■ link sounds to letters.'

RATIONALE

Part A
The child should have been given opportunities during the teaching of **Step 1** to copy and continue rhyming strings. Part A of **Step 2** tests his ability to do this.

Simple monosyllabic words and 'nonsense words' are used with familiar rhyming patterns. The child may give either or both as responses, as it is the child's ability to hear and say rhymes that is tested, not his comprehension or vocabulary.

Part B – Hearing
The child is asked to listen to a word spoken by the teacher and identify its initial phoneme. Simple monosyllabic words have been chosen.

The phonemes **s m c/k t g h** are tested.

Part C – Saying
The child looks at a picture and says the initial phoneme aloud. Easily identifiable pictures representing monosyllabic words have been chosen.

The phonemes **s m c/k t g h** are tested.

Part D – Reading
The child looks at a line of three possible words and points to the word that begins with the grapheme spoken by the teacher.

The words from which the child selects have been deliberately chosen:
- to be real words;
- to reflect a variety of letter shapes;
- as monosyllabic;
- as phonically regular;
- as rhymes, so the child can focus on the initial phoneme/grapheme.

The graphemes **s m c t g h** are tested.

Part E – Writing
The child looks again at the pictures in Part B and writes each initial grapheme.

ADMINISTRATION

Group size
The **Step 2** assessments have to be administered individually, as they have 'hearing' and 'saying' parts.

Timing
Individual children's response times will vary, but 10 minutes per child is usually sufficient to complete all parts.

Preparation
You will need:
- for each pupil, a copy of **Teacher Recording Sheet 2**, on which all of the child's responses can be recorded;
- Resource Sheets **2C** and **2D** – the picture sheet for Part C and the word choices sheet for Part D (both of which should ideally be photocopied onto card and laminated, for reuse);
- the **soundlist** for Part D (below).

The child will need a pencil.

TESTING THE CHILD

Part A
Explain that you are going to say some rhyming words (given on the **Teacher Recording Sheet**) and the child is to add another to the pattern.

The child's word is added to the rhyming string – nonsense words are acceptable, as it is the ability to hear and say rhymes that is being tested.

Part B
Explain that you are going to say a word (given on the **Teacher Recording Sheet**) and the child is to listen carefully and say the sound it starts with. Repeat this with the other words in Part B. Record the child's responses.

Part C
Now show picture sheet **2C** to the child and ask him to look at each picture in turn and *say the sound it starts with*. Do not tell the child what the pictures are, as he may determine the phoneme from your spoken use of the word.
Record the child's responses.

Part D

Show the word choices sheet **2D** to the child and draw his attention to the first line of three words. (It may be advisable to screen all lines except that on which the child is asked to focus.)

Refer to the soundlist for **Step 2** Part D (below), say each sound in turn, and ask the child to *point to the word that begins with that sound*. This process is continued for each line. Record the child's responses.

> **STEP 2 Part D SOUNDLIST**
>
> Line 1 's'   Line 2 'm'   Line 3 'c'   Line 4 't'
> Line 5 'g'   Line 6 ' h'

Part E

Finally, ask the child to look again at each of the pictures in Part C and to *write the first sound of each picture word*. The child could do this on a separate piece of paper, while you record his responses, or the child could write on a photocopy of the sheet.

SCORING THE STEP 2 TESTS

Possible scores
Part A: 5
Part B: 6
Part C: 6
Part D: 6
Part E: 6
Total: 29

Raw score	% score
15	52
16	55
17	59
18	62
19	66
20	69
21	72
22	76
23	79

Raw score	% score
24	83
25	86
26	90
27	93
28	97
29	100

STEP THREE

> **National Literacy Strategy** – Reception; Year 1, Term 2
> **Early Learning Goals:**
> ■ 'hear and say initial and final sounds in words;
> ■ link sounds to letters.'

RATIONALE

Part A – Hearing
The child is asked to listen to a word spoken by the teacher and identify its final phoneme. Simple monosyllabic words have been chosen.

The phonemes **s m k t g** are tested.

Part B – Saying
The child looks at a picture and says the final phoneme aloud. Easily identifiable pictures representing monosyllabic words have been chosen.

The phonemes **s m k t g** are tested.

Part C – Reading
The child looks at a line of three possible words and points to the word that ends with the grapheme spoken by the teacher.

The words from which the child selects have been deliberately chosen:
- to reflect a variety of letter shapes;
- as monosyllabic;
- as phonically regular;
- as the medial vowel is the same in each word, to encourage the child to look closely at the consonants being tested.

The graphemes **ss m ck t g** are tested.

Part D – Writing
The child looks at the pictures in Part D and writes each final grapheme.

Part E – Hearing
The child is asked to listen to a word spoken by the teacher and identify its initial phoneme. Simple monosyllabic words have been chosen.

The phonemes **l n d sh ch** are tested.

Part F – Saying
The child looks at a picture and says the initial phoneme aloud. Easily identifiable pictures representing monosyllabic words have been chosen.

The phonemes **l n d sh ch** are tested.

Part G – Reading
The child looks at a line of three possible words and points to the word that begins with the grapheme spoken by the teacher.

The words from which the child selects have been deliberately chosen:
- to reflect a variety of letter shapes;
- as monosyllabic;
- as phonically regular;
- to rhyme – so the child can focus on the initial phoneme/grapheme.

The graphemes **l n d k sh ch** are tested.

Part H – Writing
The child looks at the pictures and writes each initial grapheme.

Part I – Hearing
The child is asked to listen to a word spoken by the teacher and identify its final phoneme. Simple monosyllabic words have been chosen.

The phonemes **ll n d sh ch** are tested.

Part J – Saying
The child looks at a picture and says the final phoneme aloud. Easily identifiable pictures representing monosyllabic words have been chosen.

The phonemes **ll n d sh ch** are tested.

Part K – Reading
The child looks at a line of three possible words and points to the word spoken by the teacher that ends with that grapheme.

The word from which the child selects have been deliberately chosen:
- to reflect a variety of letter shapes;
- as monosyllabic;
- as phonically regular;
- as having the same Consonant-Vowel beginnings – so the

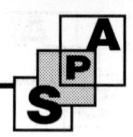

child has to distinguish only the final phoneme/grapheme.

The graphemes **ll n d sh ch** are tested.

Part L – Writing
The child looks at the pictures and writes each final grapheme.

ADMINISTRATION

Group size
The **Step 3** test has to be administered individually, as the test has 'hearing' and 'saying' parts.

Timing
Individual children's response times will vary, but 25 minutes per child is usually sufficient time to complete all parts.

Preparation
You will need:
- for each pupil, a copy of **Teacher Recording Sheets 3.1–3.3**, on which all of the child's responses can be recorded;
- Resource Sheets **3B–3D, 3F–3H** and **3J–3L** – the picture sheets for Parts B, D, F, H, J and L, and the word choices sheets for Parts C, G, and K (all of which should ideally be photocopied onto card and laminated, for reuse);
- the **soundlists** for Parts C, G and K.

The child will need a pencil.

TESTING THE CHILD

Part A
Explain that you are going to say a word (given on the **Teacher Recording Sheet**) and the child is to listen carefully and *say the sound it ends with*. Repeat this with the other words in Part A. Record the child's responses.

Part B
Show picture sheet **3B** to the child and ask him to look at each picture in turn and *say the sound it ends with*. Do not tell the child what the picture is, as he may determine the final phoneme from your spoken use of the word. Record the child's responses.

Part C
Now show the word choices sheet **3C** to the child and draw his attention to the first line of three words. (It may be advisable to screen all lines except that on which the child is asked to focus.)

Refer to the soundlist below, say each sound in turn, and ask the child to *point to the word that ends with that sound*. Continue the process for each line.

> **STEP 3 Part C SOUNDLIST**
> Line 1 's'   Line 2 'm'   Line 3 'k'   Line 4 't'   Line 5 'g'

Part D
Ask the child to look at each picture on picture sheet **3D** and write its ending sound. This may be done on a separate piece of paper. Record the child's responses.

Part E
Explain that you are going to say a word (given on the **Teacher Recording Sheet**) and that the child is to listen carefully and *say the sound it starts with*. Repeat this with the other words in Part E. Record the child's responses.

Part F
Now show picture sheet **3F** to the child and ask him to look at each picture in turn and *say the sound it starts with*. Record the child's responses.

Part G
Show the word choices sheet **3G** to the child and draw his attention to the first line of three words. (Screen other lines if necessary.) Refer to the soundlist below, say each sound in turn, and ask the child to *point to the word that starts with that sound*. Continue the process with the other lines of words. Record the child's responses.

> **STEP 3 Part G SOUNDLIST**
> Line 1 'l'   Line 2 'n'   Line 3 'd'   Line 4 'k'
> Line 5 'sh'   Line 6 'ch'

Part H
Now show picture sheet **3H** to the child and ask him to look at each picture in turn and *write the sound it starts with*. This may be done on a separate sheet of paper. Record the child's responses.

Part I
Explain that you are going to say a word (given on the **Teacher Recording Sheet**) and that the child is to listen carefully and *say the sound it ends with*. Repeat this with the other words in Part I. Record the child's responses.

Part J
Now show picture sheet **3J** to the child and ask him to look at each picture in turn and *say the sound it ends with*. Record the child's responses.

Part K
Show the word choices sheet **3K** to the child and ask him to look at the first line of three words. (Screen the other lines if necessary.) Refer to the **soundlist** below, say each sound in turn, and ask the child to *point to the word that ends with the sound*. Continue the process with the other lines. Record the child's responses.

STEP 3 Part K SOUNDLIST		
Line 1 'l'	Line 2 'n'	Line 3 'd'
Line 4 'sh'	Line 5 'ch'	

Part L
Finally, show picture sheet **3L** to the child and ask him to look at each picture in turn and *write the sound it ends with* on a separate sheet of paper. Record the child's responses.

SCORING THE STEP 3 TESTS

Possible scores
Part A: 5
Part B: 5
Part C: 5
Part D: 5
Part E: 5
Part F: 5
Part G: 6
Part H: 6
Part I: 5
Part J: 5
Part K: 5
Part L: 5
Total: 62

Raw score	% score
31	50
32	52
33	53
34	55
35	56
36	58
37	60
38	61
39	63
40	65
41	66
42	68
43	69
44	71
45	73
46	74
47	76
48	77
49	79

Raw score	% score
50	81
51	82
52	84
53	86
54	87
55	89
56	90
57	92
58	94
59	95
60	97
61	98
62	100

STEP FOUR

> National Literacy Strategy – Reception; Year 1, Terms 1, 2
> Early Learning Goals:
> - 'hear and say initial and final sounds in words, and short vowel sounds within words;
> - link sounds to letters;
> - use their phonic knowledge to write simple regular words.'

RATIONALE

Part A – Hearing
The child is asked to listen to a word spoken by the teacher and identify its medial phoneme. Simple monosyllabic, Consonant-Vowel-Consonant words have been chosen.

The phonemes **a e i o u** are tested.

Part B – Saying
The child looks at a picture and says the medial phoneme aloud. Easily identifiable pictures representing monosyllabic words have been chosen.

The phonemes **a e i o u** are tested.

Part C – Reading
The child looks at a line of three possible words and circles the word spoken by the teacher that has the medial grapheme.

The words from which the child selects have been deliberately chosen:
- to have the same initial consonant;
- to have the same final consonant

– so the child has to focus only on the medial vowel.

The graphemes **a e i o u** are tested.

Part D – Writing
The child looks at the pictures in Part D and writes each medial grapheme.

Part E – Hearing
The child is asked to listen to a word spoken by the teacher and identify its initial phoneme. Simple monosyllabic words have been chosen.

The phonemes **f qu b r j p th** are tested.

Part F – Saying
The child looks at a picture and says the initial phoneme aloud. Easily identifiable pictures representing monosyllabic words have been chosen.

The phonemes **f qu b r j p th** are tested.

Part G – Reading
The child looks at a line of three possible words and circles the word spoken by the teacher that begins with the grapheme. The words from which the child selects have been deliberately chosen to rhyme, so the child can focus on the initial consonant.

The graphemes **f qu b r j p th** are tested.

Part H – Writing
The child looks at the pictures and writes each initial grapheme.

Part I – Hearing
The child is asked to listen to a word spoken by the teacher and identify its final phoneme. Simple monosyllabic words have been chosen.

The phonemes **ff b p th ng** are tested.

Part J – Saying
The child looks at a picture and says the final phoneme aloud. Easily identifiable pictures representing monosyllabic words have been chosen.

The phonemes **ff b p th ng** are tested.

Part K – Reading
The child looks at a line of three possible words and circles the word spoken by the teacher that ends with that grapheme. The words from which the child selects have been chosen to have the same initial Consonant-Vowel, so the child can focus on the final grapheme.

The graphemes **ff b p th ng** are tested.

Part L – Writing
The child looks at the pictures and writes each final grapheme.

Part M – Spelling
The child completes a series of simple sentences with a dictated Consonant-Vowel-Consonant word.

Part N – Reading

The child chooses, from three words, the word dictated by the teacher.

The three words from which the child selects have been carefully chosen:
- All three words have graphic similarities – two of the three may have the same initial consonant; or the same final consonant; or the same rime. This is to encourage the child to read each word carefully before making a choice.
- All three words are real words, many of which will already be familiar to the child.
- All the words are phonically regular.

ADMINISTRATION

Group size
Parts A to L of the **Step 4** test have to be administered to an individual child, as these parts have 'hearing' and 'saying' parts.

Parts M and N can be administered to a group or class.

Timing
Individual children's response times will vary, but 25 minutes per child is usually sufficient time to complete **Parts A to L**.

Part M will take approximately 15 minutes; **Part N** will take approximately 10 minutes.

Preparation
You will need:
- for each pupil, a copy of **Teacher Recording Sheets 4.1–4.3**, on which the child's responses can be recorded;
- Resource Sheets **4B–4D, 4F–4H** and **4J–4L** – the picture sheets for Parts B, D, F, H, J and L, and the word choice sheets for Parts C, G and K (all of which should ideally be photocopied onto card and laminated, for reuse);
- a copy of the **wordlists** for Parts M and N for the spelling and reading contextual sentences.

The child will need:
- a copy of Test Sheets **4M** and **4N**, on which to write the words;
- a pencil (and a rubber if this is normal practice).

TESTING THE CHILD

Part A
Explain that you are going to say a word (given on the **Teacher Recording Sheet**) and the child is to listen carefully and *say the sound in the middle of the word*. Repeat this with the other words in Part A. Record the child's responses.

Part B
Now show picture sheet **4B** to the child and ask him to look at each picture in turn and *say its middle sound*. Do not tell the child what the pictures are, as he may determine the phoneme from your spoken use of the word. Record the child's responses.

Part C
Show the word choices sheet **4C** to the child and draw his attention to the first line of three words. (It may be advisable to screen all lines except that on which the child is asked to focus.)

Refer to the **soundlist** below, say each sound in turn, and ask the child to *point to the word that has that middle sound*. This process is continued for each line. Record the child's responses.

> **STEP 4 Part C SOUNDLIST**
> Line 1 '**a**'   Line 2 '**e**'   Line 3 '**i**'   Line 4 '**o**'   Line 5 '**u**'

Part D
Ask the child to look at each of the pictures on picture sheet **4D** and to *write its middle sound*. This may be done on a separate piece of paper. Record the child's responses.

Part E
Explain that you are going to say a word (given on the **Teacher Recording Sheet**) and that the child is to listen carefully and *say the sound it starts with*. Repeat this with the other words in Part E. Record the child's responses.

Part F
Now show picture sheet **4F** to the child and ask him to look at each picture in turn and *say the sound it starts with*. Record the child's responses.

Part G
Show the word choices sheet **4G** to the child and draw his attention to the first line of three words. (Screen the other lines if necessary.) Refer to the **soundlist** below, say each

sound in turn, and ask the child to *point to the word that starts with that sound*. Continue the process with the other lines of words. Record the child's responses.

> **STEP 4 Part G SOUNDLIST**
> Line 1 'f'   Line 2 'qu'   Line 3 'b'   Line 4 'r'   Line 5 'j'
> Line 6 'p'   Line 7 'th'

Part H
Now show picture sheet **4H** to the child and ask him to look at each picture in turn and *write the sound it starts with*. This may be done on a separate piece of paper. Record the child's responses.

Part I
Explain that you are going to say a word (given on the **Teacher Recording Sheet**) and that the child is to listen carefully and *say the sound it ends with*. Repeat with the other words in Part I. Record the child's responses.

Part J
Show picture sheet **4J** to the child and ask him to look at each picture in turn and *say the sound it ends with*. Record the child's responses.

Part K
Now show the word choices sheet **4K** to the child and ask him to look at the first line of three words. (Screen the other words if necessary.) Refer to the **soundlist** below, say each sound in turn, and ask the child to *point to the word that ends with that sound*. Continue the process with the other lines. Record the child's responses.

> **STEP 4 Part K SOUNDLIST**
> Line 1 'f'   Line 2 'b'   Line 3 'p'   Line 4 'th'   Line 5 'ng'

Part L
Show picture sheet **4L** to the child and ask him to look at each picture in turn and *write the sound it ends with*. This may be done on a separate piece of paper. Record the child's responses.

Now refer to the wordlist for Parts M & N, given below in completed sentences to ensure the correct words are dictated.

Part M
The child needs a copy of Test Sheets **4M**. You read each sentence aloud – including the target word. You then repeat the target word, and instruct the child to *write the word on the line*:

eg: You read *'I hit the ball with a bat.'*
    And then repeat *'bat'*; and say *'Write <u>bat</u> on the line.'*

Part N

The child needs a copy of Test Sheets **4N**. You read each sentence aloud – including the target word. Then repeat the target word and instruct the child to read (silently or aloud) the three words and *circle the target word*.

eg: You read *'I hit the ball with a bat.'*
    And then repeat *'bat'*; and say *'Look carefully at the three words and put a circle around the word <u>bat</u>'*.

STEP 4 WORDLIST for Parts M & N
1. I hit the ball with a __**bat**__ .
2. A boy grows up into a __**man**__ .
3. Unkind people make me __**sad**__ .
4. I like __**ham**__ sandwiches.
5. I can hop on one __**leg**__ .
6. Five and five make __**ten**__ .
7. I have a __**pet**__ dog.
8. __**Red**__ is a bright colour.
9. A __**bib**__ keeps a baby clean.
10. I like to __**win**__ races.
11. Please __**sit**__ still on the carpet.
12. A __**pip**__ is a small seed.
13. We use a __**rod**__ to catch fish.
14. I do __**not**__ like creepy-crawlies.
15. I like to __**jog**__ to keep fit.
16. Frogs can __**hop**__ on lily pads.
17. It is __**fun**__ to play games.
18. We use scissors to __**cut**__ paper.
19. I __**dug**__ a hole with a spade.
20. Pigs like to roll in the __**mud**__ .

SCORING THE STEP 4 TESTS

Possible scores
Part A: 5
Part B: 5
Part C: 5
Part D: 5
Part E: 7
Part F: 7
Part G: 7
Part H: 7
Part I: 5
Part J: 5
Part K: 5
Part L: 5
Part M: 20
Part N: 20
Total: 108

Raw score	% score
54	50
55	51
56	52
57	53
58	54
59	55
60	56
61	57
62	57
63	58
64	59
65	60
67	62
68	63
69	64
70	65
71	66
72	67
73	68
74	69
75	69
76	70
77	71
78	72
79	73
80	74
81	75
82	76
83	77
84	78
85	79

Raw score	% score
86	80
87	81
88	81
89	82
90	82
91	83
92	84
93	85
94	86
95	88
96	89
97	90
98	91
99	92
100	93
101	94
102	94
103	95
104	96
105	97
106	98
107	99
108	100

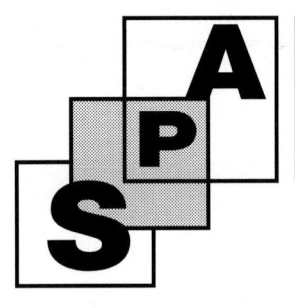

STEP FIVE

> **National Literacy Strategy** – Reception; Year 1, Terms 1, 2
> **Early Learning Goals:**
> - 'hear and say initial and final sounds in words;
> - link sounds to letters;
> - use their phonic knowledge to write simple regular words.'

RATIONALE

Step 5 appears to be the same length as **Step 4** in *Progression in Phonics*, but, as in Year 1, Term 2, of the Appendix to the National Literacy Strategy, there are a considerable number of initial and final consonant clusters to be covered. There are also the remaining single consonants to complete.

Part A – Hearing
The child is asked to listen to a word spoken by the teacher and identify its initial/final phoneme. Simple, monosyllabic words have been chosen.

The phonemes **v w y z x** are tested.

Part B – Saying
The child looks at a picture and says the initial/final phoneme aloud. Easily identifiable pictures representing monosyllabic words have been chosen.

The phonemes **v w y z x** are tested.

Part C – Reading
The child looks at a line of three possible words and circles the word spoken by the teacher that has the initial/final grapheme.

The words from which the child selects have been deliberately chosen to rhyme (**v, w, y, z**), so the child has to focus only on the initial grapheme. The choices for the **x** grapheme have the same initial consonant and medial vowel.

The graphemes **v w y z x** are tested.

Part D – Writing
The child looks at the pictures in Part B and writes each initial/final grapheme.

Part E – Hearing
The child is asked to listen to a word spoken by the teacher and identify its initial consonant cluster.

Simple monosyllabic words have been chosen.

The clusters **bl br cl cr dr dw fl fr gl gr pl pr sc scr sk sl sm sn sp spl spr squ st str sw tr tw thr shr** are tested.

Part F – Saying
The child looks at a picture and says the initial consonant cluster aloud. Easily identifiable pictures representing monosyllabic words have been chosen.

The clusters **bl br cl cr dr fl fr gl gr pl pr sc scr sk sl sm sn sp squ st sw tr tw thr** are tested.

Part G – Hearing
The child is asked to listen to a word spoken by the teacher and identify the final consonant cluster. Simple, monosyllabic words have been chosen.

The clusters **ld nd lk nk sk lp mp sp ct ft lt nt pt st xt lf nch lth** are tested.

Part H – Saying
The child looks at a picture and says the final consonant cluster aloud. Easily identifiable pictures representing simple, monosyllabic words have been chosen.

The clusters **ld nd lk nk sk lt nt st lf nch** are tested.

Part I – Spelling
The child completes a series of simple sentences with a dictated Consonant-Consonant-Vowel-Consonant word.

Part J – Reading
The child chooses, from three words, the word dictated by the teacher.

The three words from which the child selects have been deliberately chosen to have graphic similarities – two or three of the words may have the same initial consonant cluster; or the same final consonant; or the same medial vowel; or the same rime. This is to encourage the child to read each word carefully before making a choice.

Wherever possible, real words have been used, many of which will already be familiar to the child. All the words are phonically regular.

Part K – Spelling
The child completes a series of simple sentences with a dictated Consonant-Vowel-Consonant-Consonant word.

Part L – Reading
The child chooses, from the three words, the word dictated by the teacher.

The three words from which the child selects have been deliberately chosen to have graphic similarities – all of the words have the same initial consonant and vowel. This is to encourage the child to read the final cluster carefully.

Wherever possible, real words have been used, many of which will be familiar to the child. All the words are phonically regular.

ADMINISTRATION

Group size
Parts A to H of the **Step 5** test have to be administered individually, as these parts have 'hearing' and 'saying' parts.

Parts I to L can be administered to a group or class.

Timing
Individual children's response times will vary, but 25 minutes per child is usually sufficient time to complete **Parts A to H**.

Part I will take approximately 15 minutes; **Part J** will take approximately 10 minutes; **Part K** will take approximately 15 minutes; **Part L** will take approximately 10 minutes.

Preparation
You will need:
- for each pupil, a copy of **Teacher Recording Sheets 5.1–5.3**, on which the child's responses can be recorded;
- Resource Sheets **5B–5D**, **5F** and **5H** – the picture sheets for Parts B, D, F and H, and the word choice sheet for Parts C (all of which should ideally be photocopied onto card and laminated, for reuse);
- a copy of the **wordlists** for Parts I–L for the spelling and reading contextual sentences.

The child will need:
- copies of Test Sheets **5I–5L**, on which to write the words;
- a pencil (and a rubber if this is normal practice).

TESTING THE CHILD

Part A
Explain that you are going to say a word (given on the **Teacher Recording Sheet**) and the child is to listen carefully

and say the sound at the start (**v, w, y, z**) or end of the word (**x**). Record the child's responses.

Part B
Now show picture sheet **5B** to the child and ask him to look at each picture in turn and *say its start/end sound*. Do not tell the child what the pictures are, as he may determine the phoneme from your spoken use of the word. Record the child's responses.

Part C
Show the word choices sheet **5C** to the child and draw his attention to the first line of three words. (It may be advisable to screen all lines except that on which the child is asked to focus.) Refer to the **soundlist** below, say each sound in turn, and ask the child to *point to the word that has the start (v, w, y, z) / end (x) sound*.

Continue this process for each line. Record the child's responses.

STEP 5 Part C SOUNDLIST
Line 1 'v'   Line 'w'   Line 3 'y'   Line 4 'z'   Line 5 'x'

Part D
Ask the child to look again at each of the pictures on picture sheet **5B** and to *write the initial (v, w, y, z) / end (x) sound*. This may be done on a separate piece of paper. Record the child's responses.

Part E
Explain that you are going to say a word (given on the **Teacher Recording Sheet**) and that the child is to listen carefully and *say the sound it starts with*. Repeat this with the other words in Part E. Record the child's responses.

Part F
Now show picture sheet **5F** to the child and ask him to look at each picture in turn and *say the sound it starts with*. Record the child's responses.

Part G
Explain that you are going to say a word (given on the **Teacher Recording Sheet**) and that the child is to listen carefully and *say the sound it ends with*. Repeat this with the other words in Part G. Record the child's responses.

Part H
Now show picture sheet **5H** to the child and ask him to look at each picture in turn and *say the sound it ends with*. Record the child's responses.

Now refer to the wordlists for Parts I & J, and K & L, given below in completed sentences to ensure the correct words are dictated.

STEP 5 WORDLIST for Parts I & J

1. The darkest colour is __black__ .
2. __Bricks__ are used to build houses.
3. I can __clap__ my hands.
4. A __crab__ walks sideways.
5. We can bang a __drum__ .
6. A square is a __flat__ shape.
7. A __frog__ hops into a pond.
8. I am so __glad__ you've come to tea.
9. My __gran__ is an old lady.
10. A __plum__ is a juicy, purple fruit.
11. A baby rides in a __pram__ .
12. Put the rubbish on the __scrap__ heap.
13. My __skin__ is soft and smooth.
14. Don't __slip__ on the icy road.
15. Don't __smash__ the window!
16. Scissors can __snip__ paper.
18. I like to __swim__ in the water.
17. Can you __spot__ the mistake?
19. In __spring__ the birds build their nests.
20. A red light means __stop__ .
21. We had to __strap__ the baby in the car seat.
22. I like to __splash__ in the pool.
23. We went on a school __trip__ .
24. I wish I had a __twin__ sister.
25. It is rude to __shrug__ your shoulders.

STEP 5 WORDLIST for Parts K & L

1. __Hold__ on tight to the rail.
2. There is a __bend__ in the road.
3. __Milk__ comes from cows.
4. __Pink__ is a pretty colour.
5. The old elephant had lost a __tusk__ .
6. __Help__ me! I'm falling.
7. Ouch! We rode over a __bump__ .
8. The apple was __crisp__ and juicy.
9. The girl wanted to __act__ on the stage.
10. My aunt sent me a birthday __gift__ .
11. The ice-cream began to __melt__ in the sun.
12. We __went__ for a walk.
13. I __swept__ up the crumbs.
14. I got __lost__ in the fog.
15. You are __next__ in the queue.
16. Can you reach the top __shelf__ ?
17. I had sandwiches in my packed __lunch__ .
18. Can you __catch__ the ball?

Parts I & K

The child needs copies of Test Sheets **5I** and **5K**.

You read each sentence aloud – including the target word. You then repeat the target word and instruct the child to write the word on the line.

eg: 'You read *The darkest colour is black.*'
And then repeat '*black,*' and say '*Write black on the line.*'

Parts J & L

The child needs copies of Test Sheets **5J** and **5L**.

You read each sentence aloud – including the target word. Then repeat the target word and instruct the child to read (silently or aloud) the three words and circle the target word.
eg: You read *'The darkest colour is black.'*
     And then repeat *'black,'* and say *'Look carefully at the three words and put a circle around the word* black.*'*

SCORING THE STEP 5 TESTS

Possible scores
Part A: 5
Part B: 5
Part C: 5
Part D: 5
Part E: 29
Part F: 24
Part G: 18
Part H: 10
Part I: 25
Part J: 25
Part K: 18
Part L: 18
Total: 187

Raw Score	% score	Raw Score	% score
93-94	50	149-150	80
95-96	51	151-152	81
97-98	52	153-154	82
99-100	53	155-156	83
101	54	157-158	84
102-103	55	159	85
104-105	56	160-161	86
106-107	57	162-163	87
108-109	58	164-165	88
110-111	59	166-167	89
112-113	60	168-169	90
114-115	61	170-171	91
116	62	172-173	92
117-118	63	174	93
119-120	64	175-176	94
121-122	65	177-178	95
123-124	66	179-180	96
125-126	67	181-182	97
127-128	68	183-184	98
129	69	185-186	99
130-131	70	187	100
132-133	71		
134-135	72		
136-137	73		
138-139	74		
140-141	75		
142-143	76		
144-145	77		
146	78		
147-148	79		

STEP SIX

National Literacy Strategy – Year 1, Term 3; Year 2, Term 1

RATIONALE

Step 6 concentrates on ten representations of vowel phonemes. The test words have been specifically chosen to reflect the most common graphic patterns. (These can be found on the *Progression in Phonics* CD-ROM.)

Parts A and B focus on the five most common representations of the long-vowel phonemes – **ai ee ie oa oo**.

Parts C and D focus on the vowel phonemes – **or ar ir oi ou**.

Parts A & C – Spelling
The child completes a series of simple sentences with a dictated Consonant-Vowel digraph-Consonant word.

Parts B & D – Reading
All the 'words' in the reading test are phonetically plausible and the child must be familiar with the most common convention in order to eliminate the incorrect answers.

ADMINISTRATION

Group size
The **Step 6** tests can be administered to a group or class.

Timing
It may be advisable to use **Parts A and B** in one session, and **Parts C and D** in a later session.

Part A will take approximately 10 minutes; **Part B** will take approximately 15 minutes; **Part C** will take approximately 10 minutes; **Part D** will take approximately 15 minutes.

The time taken to complete each test will be less once the child is familiar with the routine.

Preparation
You will need to refer to the Parts A, B, C and D **wordlists** (below) for the spelling and reading contextual sentences.

The child will need:
- Test Sheets **6A–6D**, on which to write the words;
- a pencil (and a rubber if this is normal practice).

TESTING THE CHILD

Parts A & C
You read each sentence aloud – including the target word. You then repeat the target word and instruct the child to write the word on the line.
eg: You read '*I paid for my shopping.*'
    And then repeat '*paid,*' and say '*Write paid on the line.*'

Parts B & D
You read each sentence aloud – including the target word. Then repeat the target word and instruct the child to read (silently or aloud) the three words and circle the target word.
eg: You read '*I paid for my shopping.*'
    And then repeat '*paid,*' and say '*Look carefully at the three words and put a circle around the word paid.*'

STEP 6 WORDLIST for Parts A & B

1. I __paid__ for my shopping.
2. A ship __sails__ on the sea.
3. I had a __pain__ in my leg.
4. Plant the __seed__ in the ground.
5. There are seven days in a __week__ .
6. How do you __feel__ today?
7. Where have you __been__ ?
8. The water is very __deep__ .
9. Will you __meet__ me later?
10. I love apple __pie__ and custard.
11. The little boy __tied__ his laces.
12. The main __road__ had a lot of traffic.
13. The footballer scored a __goal__ .
14. Wash your hands with __soap__ .
15. Put your __coat__ on, it's cold outside.
16. The builders mended the __roof__ .
17. It is __cool__ in the shade.
18. The __room__ was clean and tidy.
19. The __moon__ shone brightly at night.
20. The plant had a very long __root__ .

STEP 6 WORDLIST for Parts C & D
1. Some people use a knife and __fork__ to eat.
2. The baby was __born__ in the hospital.
3. Could you please __sort__ it out?
4. The children all worked very __hard__.
5. The family went for a walk in the __park__.
6. "Old MacDonald had a __farm__."
7. The owl flew into the __barn__.
8. __Sharp__ scissors cut better.
9. A wheel is __part__ of a car.
10. The __bird__ made a nest.
11. My sister is a little __girl__.
12. Your shoes are covered in __dirt__!
13. A kettle will __boil__ water.
14. I'd like to __join__ the recorder club.
15. Please don't __shout__ at me.

SCORING THE STEP 6 TESTS

Possible scores
Part A: 20
Part B: 20
Part C: 15
Part D: 15
Total: 70

Raw Score	% score	Raw Score	% score
35	50	56	80
36	51	57	81
37	53	58	83
38	54	59	84
39	56	60	86
40	57	61	87
41	59	62	89
42	60	63	90
43	61	64	91
44	63	65	93
45	64	66	94
46	66	67	96
47	67	68	97
48	69	69	99
49	70	70	100
50	71		
51	73		
52	74		
53	76		
54	77		
55	79		

STEP SEVEN

National Literacy Strategy – Year 1, Term 3; Year 2, Terms 1, 2, 3

RATIONALE

Step 7 is a long step that concentrates on nineteen representations of vowel phonemes. The test words have been specifically chosen to reflect the most common graphic patterns. (These can be found on the *Progression in Phonics* CD-ROM.)

Parts A and B focus on the eleven common representations of the long-vowel phonemes – **ay a-e ea igh y i-e o-e oe ew ue u-e.**

Parts C and D focus on the eight vowel phonemes – **oy ow er ur aw air ear oo.**

Parts A & C – Spelling
The child completes a series of simple sentences with a dictated:
- Consonant-Vowel digraph-Consonant word; *or*
- Consonant-Vowel digraph/trigraph word; *or*
- Consonant cluster-Vowel digraph-Consonant word.

Parts B & D – Reading
All the 'words' in the reading test are phonetically plausible and the child must be familiar with the most common and likely convention in order to eliminate the incorrect answers.

ADMINISTRATION

Group size
The **Step 7** tests can be administered to a group or class.

Timing
It may be advisable to use Parts A and B of the test on separate occasions because of their length.

Part A will take approximately 30 minutes; **Part B** will take approximately 30 minutes; **Part C** will take approximately 15 minutes; **Part D** will take approximately 10 minutes.

The time taken to complete each test will be less once the child is familiar with the routine.

Preparation
You will need to refer to the A, B, C and D **wordlists** (below)

for the spelling and reading contextual sentences.
The child will need:
- copies of Test Sheets **7A–7D**, on which to write the words;
- a pencil (and a rubber if this is normal practice).

TESTING THE CHILD

Parts A & C
You read each sentence aloud including the target word. You then repeat the target word and instruct the child to write the word on the line.
eg: You read *'I made a model.'*
And then repeat *'made,'* and say *'Write <u>made</u> on the line.'*

Parts B & D
You read each sentence aloud – including the target word. Then repeat the target word and instruct the child to read (silently or aloud) the three words and *circle the target word*.
eg: You read *'I made a model.'*
And then repeat *'made,'* and say *'Look carefully at the three words and put a circle around the word <u>made</u>.'*

STEP 7 WORDLIST for Parts A & B

1. Pardon, what did you **say**?
2. Is this the right **way**?
3. I **made** a model.
4. The bird was kept in a **cage**.
5. The birthday **cake** had six candles.
6. This house is for **sale**.
7. What is your **name**?
8. A circle is a round **shape**.
9. Close the **gate** behind you.
10. I **save** up my pocket money.
11. I like to **read** books.
12. A **leaf** is part of a plant.
13. It's your turn to **deal** the cards.
14. I was picked to play in the football **team**.
15. Sorry, I didn't **mean** it.
16. Things are **cheap** if they don't cost much money.
17. The fire gave out a lot of **heat**.
18. At midday the sun is **high** in the sky.
19. It's dark, switch on the **light**.
20. I am kind and share **my** toys.
21. "Three blind **mice**" is a well-known rhyme.
22. I can **ride** a bike.
23. In Spring the trees seem to come to **life**.
24. I **like** to have fun.
25. Put your books in a tidy **pile**.
26. Is it nearly dinner **time**?
27. Give that back, it's **mine**!
28. **Wipe** your dirty feet!
29. Can you **dive** into the pool?
30. I **rode** my bike down the hill.
31. That is a funny **joke**.
32. Don't fall down the **hole**!
33. I want to go **home**!
34. The dog chews the **bone**.
35. I **hope** I get this right!
36. A **rose** is a lovely scented flower.
37. Who will you **vote** for?
38. Someone stood on my **toe**.
39. The seeds **grew** into plants.
40. The sky looks **blue** on a sunny day.
41. It is **rude** to stare.
42. An elephant is a **huge** animal.
43. I can play a **tune** on the piano.
44. An electric plug has a **fuse**.
45. The little baby looked very **cute**.

STEP 7 WORDLIST for Parts C & D

1. A _boy_ grows up into a man.
2. The dog began to _howl_.
3. A _town_ has many shops.
4. How high can you _throw_ a ball?
5. The seeds had _grown_ into plants.
6. A group of cattle is called a _herd_.
7. We have a holiday at half-_term_.
8. The baby's hair began to _curl_.
9. Ouch! I _hurt_ myself.
10. A _hawk_ is a bird of prey.
11. The baby learns to _crawl_.
12. Please sit on the _chair_.
13. Pardon, I didn't _hear_ you.
14. The children were very _good_.
15. The _book_ is very interesting to read.

SCORING THE STEP 7 TESTS

Possible scores

Part A: 45
Part B: 45
Part C: 15
Part D: 15
Total: 120

Raw Score	% score
60	50
61	51
62	52
63-64	53
65	54
66	55
67	56
68	57
69-70	58
71	59
72	60
73	61
74	62
75-76	63
77	64
78	65
79	66
80	67
81-82	68
83	69
84	70
85	71
86	72
87-88	73
89	74
90	75

Raw Score	% score
91	76
92	77
93-94	78
95	79
96	80
97	81
98	82
99-100	83
101	84
102	85
103	86
104	87
105-106	88
107	89
108	90
109	91
110	92
111-112	93
113	94
114	95
115	96
116	97
117-118	98
119	99
120	100

Step 1

Teacher Recording Sheet 1

Name_____ Date_____ Assessed by_____

General sound discrimination

Can recognise sounds in the environment
(using taped sounds – e.g. traffic, children/adults speaking, computers humming, clocks ticking – everyday sounds which will be familiar to the child at home and at school) ☐

Can recognise instrumental sounds
(using musical instruments – e.g. banging a drum, plucking strings, shaking a tambourine, and sounds such as clapping, stamping, etc, made using our own bodies) ☐

Speech/sound discrimination

Joins in with voice games to produce phonemes ☐

Rhythm and rhyme

Joins in with rhyming games ☐

Alliteration

Joins in with alliterative games ☐

Steps in Phonics Assessment is published by Hodder & Stoughton Educational. The publishers grant permission for photocopies of this sheet to be made for use solely in the purchasing institution.

Step 2

Teacher Recording Sheet 2

Name_____ Date_____ Assessed by_____

A. Can orally continue the rhyming string (*teacher reads*).

bat	wat	fat	_____	☐
hen	den	len	_____	☐
mig	jig	wig	_____	☐
hot	pot	not	_____	☐
sun	vun	run	_____	☐

B. Can hear the initial phoneme of … (*teacher reads*).

<u>s</u>and ☐   <u>m</u>at ☐   <u>k</u>iss ☐   <u>t</u>ed ☐   <u>g</u>oat ☐   <u>h</u>orse ☐

C. Can say the initial phoneme of … (*child looks at picture on sheet and says sound*).

<u>s</u>un	<u>m</u>oon	<u>c</u>at	<u>t</u>ap	<u>g</u>irl	<u>h</u>ouse
☐	☐	☐	☐	☐	☐

D. Recognises the initial grapheme of the word: points to the word that starts with … (*teacher reads choices – refer to soundlist*)

pit	<u>s</u>it	lit	☐
<u>m</u>an	ban	pan	☐
dot	<u>c</u>ot	jot	☐
hip	<u>t</u>ip	sip	☐
<u>g</u>um	hum	sum	☐
not	pot	<u>h</u>ot	☐

E. Can write the initial grapheme of the pictures in C.

☐ ☐ ☐ ☐ ☐ ☐

Steps in Phonics Assessment is published by Hodder & Stoughton Educational. The publishers grant permission for photocopies of this sheet to be made for use solely in the purchasing institution.

Step 2
Picture sheet for Part C

2C

Step 2

Word choice sheet for Part D

2D

pit	sit	lit
man	ban	pan
dot	cot	jot
hip	tip	sip
gum	hum	sum
not	pot	hot

Steps in Phonics Assessment is published by Hodder & Stoughton Educational. The publishers grant permission for photocopies of this sheet to be made for use solely in the purchasing institution.

Step 3

Teacher Recording Sheet 3.1

Name_____   Date_____   Assessed by_____

A. Can hear the final phoneme of ... (*teacher reads*).

gra<u>ss</u> ☐   co<u>m</u>b ☐   lo<u>ck</u> ☐   boa<u>t</u> ☐   wi<u>g</u> ☐

B. Can say the final phoneme of ... (*child looks at picture on sheet and says sound*).

bu<u>s</u>	ja<u>m</u>	boo<u>k</u>	coa<u>t</u>	do<u>g</u>
☐	☐	☐	☐	☐

C. Recognises the final grapheme of the word: points to the word that ends with ... (*teacher reads choices – refer to soundlist*).

hi<u>ss</u>	nip	hit	☐
boot	roo<u>m</u>	soon	☐
ro<u>ck</u>	pot	log	☐
pig	dip	pi<u>t</u>	☐
rod	ho<u>g</u>	mop	☐

D. Can write the final grapheme of the picture words (*child looks at picture and writes grapheme – no help*).

dre<u>ss</u>	broo<u>m</u>	so<u>ck</u>	ba<u>t</u>	le<u>g</u>
☐	☐	☐	☐	☐

Step 3

Teacher Recording Sheet 3.2

E. Can hear the initial phoneme of ... (*teacher reads words*).

<u>l</u>og ☐   <u>n</u>ose ☐   <u>d</u>oll ☐   <u>sh</u>ip ☐   <u>ch</u>ain ☐

F. Can say the initial phoneme of ... (*child looks at picture on sheet and says sound*).

<u>l</u>amp	<u>n</u>et	<u>d</u>og	<u>sh</u>irt	<u>ch</u>ips
☐	☐	☐	☐	☐

G. Recognises the initial grapheme of the word: points to the word that begins with ... (*teacher reads choices – refer to soundlist*).

<u>l</u>eg   peg   beg   ☐

hot   <u>n</u>ot   jot   ☐

<u>d</u>ip   sip   pip   ☐

sit   <u>k</u>it   fit   ☐

stop   slop   <u>sh</u>op   ☐

<u>ch</u>op   clop   crop   ☐

H. Can write the initial grapheme of the picture words (*child looks at picture and writes grapheme – no help*).

<u>l</u>eg	<u>n</u>ine	<u>d</u>oor	<u>k</u>ing	<u>sh</u>op	<u>ch</u>air
☐	☐	☐	☐	☐	☐

Step 3

Teacher Recording Sheet 3.3

I. Can hear the final phoneme of ... (*teacher reads*).

ha<u>ll</u> ☐   pla<u>n</u> ☐   bea<u>d</u> ☐   wi<u>sh</u> ☐   ar<u>ch</u> ☐

J. Can say the final phoneme of ... (*child looks at picture on sheet and says sound*).

be<u>ll</u>	ma<u>n</u>	be<u>d</u>	fi<u>sh</u>	bea<u>ch</u>
☐	☐	☐	☐	☐

K. Recognises the final grapheme of the word: points to the word that ends with ... (*teacher reads choices – refer to soundlist*).

ten	te<u>ll</u>	tent	☐
pe<u>n</u>	pet	peg	☐
co<u>d</u>	cog	cot	☐
fist	fill	fi<u>sh</u>	☐
coats	coast	coa<u>ch</u>	☐

L. Can write the final grapheme of the picture words (*child looks at picture and writes grapheme – no help*).

ba<u>ll</u>	fa<u>n</u>	ro<u>d</u>	di<u>sh</u>	chur<u>ch</u>
☐	☐	☐	☐	☐

Steps in Phonics Assessment is published by Hodder & Stoughton Educational. The publishers grant permission for photocopies of this sheet to be made for use solely in the purchasing institution.

Step 3

Picture sheet for Part B

3B

Step 3
Word choice sheet for Part C

3C

hiss	nip	hit
boot	room	soon
rock	pot	log
pig	dip	pit
rod	hog	mop

Steps in Phonics Assessment is published by Hodder & Stoughton Educational. The publishers grant permission for photocopies of this sheet to be made for use solely in the purchasing institution.

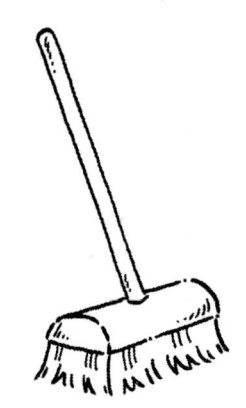

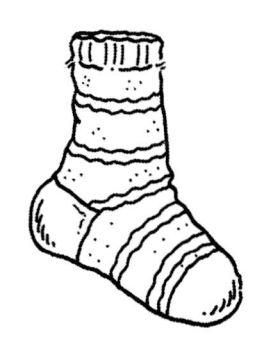

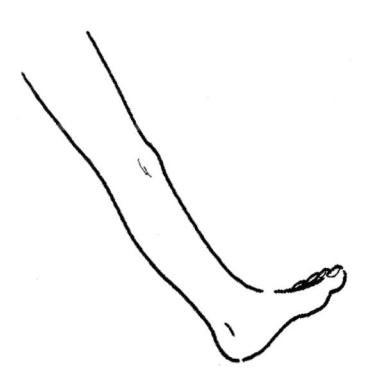

Step 3
Picture sheet for Part D

3D

Step 3
Picture sheet for Part F

3F

Step 3
Word choice sheet for Part D

3G

leg	peg	beg
hot	not	jot
dip	sip	pip
sit	kit	fit
stop	slop	shop
chop	clop	crop

Steps in Phonics Assessment is published by Hodder & Stoughton Educational. The publishers grant permission for photocopies of this sheet to be made for use solely in the purchasing institution.

Step 3
Picture sheet for Part H

3H

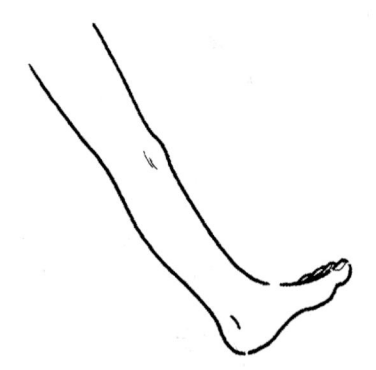

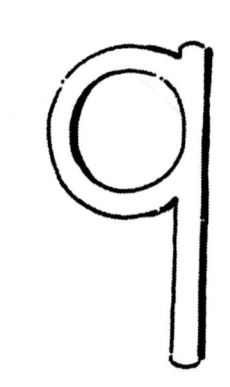

Steps in Phonics Assessment is published by Hodder & Stoughton Educational. The publishers grant permission for photocopies of this sheet to be made for use solely in the purchasing institution.

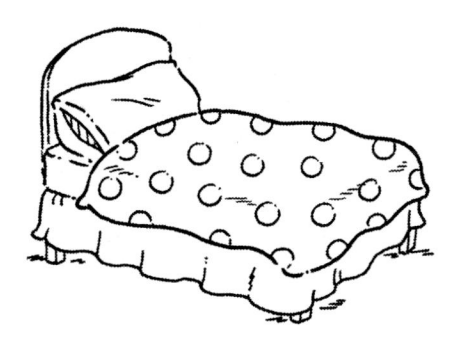

Step 3
Picture sheet for Part J

3J

Step 3

Word choice sheet for Part K

3K

ten	tell	tent
pen	pet	peg
cod	cog	cot
fist	fill	fish
coats	coast	coach

Steps in Phonics Assessment is published by Hodder & Stoughton Educational. The publishers grant permission for photocopies of this sheet to be made for use solely in the purchasing institution.

Step 3
Picture sheet for Part L

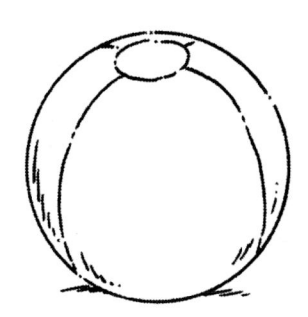

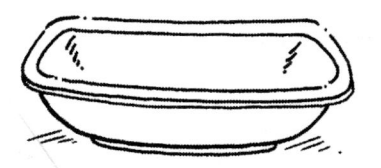

3L

Step 4

Teacher Recording Sheet 4.1

Name_____ Date_____ Assessed by_____

A. Can hear the medial phoneme of ... (*teacher reads*).

b<u>a</u>g ☐   m<u>e</u>t ☐   z<u>i</u>p ☐   p<u>o</u>d ☐   g<u>u</u>m ☐

B. Can say the medial phoneme of ... (*child looks at picture on sheet and says sound*).

| c<u>a</u>t | p<u>e</u>n | b<u>i</u>b | m<u>o</u>p | c<u>u</u>p |

C. Recognises the medial grapheme of the word: points to the word that has this sound in the middle ... (*teacher reads choices – refer to soundlist*).

pin	p<u>a</u>n	pen	☐
j<u>e</u>t	jot	jut	☐
s<u>i</u>t	set	sat	☐
pup	pip	p<u>o</u>p	☐
b<u>u</u>d	bed	bid	☐

D. Can write the medial grapheme of the picture words (*child looks at picture and writes grapheme – no help*).

| v<u>a</u>n | t<u>e</u>n | l<u>i</u>p | r<u>o</u>d | s<u>u</u>n |

☐ ☐ ☐ ☐ ☐

Step 4

Teacher Recording Sheet 4.2

E. Can hear the initial phoneme of ... (*teacher reads words*).

<u>f</u>elt ☐   <u>q</u>uiz ☐   <u>b</u>ig ☐   <u>r</u>ose ☐   <u>j</u>uice ☐   <u>p</u>iece ☐   <u>th</u>is ☐

F. Can say the initial phoneme of ... (*child looks at picture on sheet and says sound*).

<u>f</u>ish	<u>q</u>ueen	<u>b</u>all	<u>r</u>ope	<u>j</u>am	<u>p</u>ig	<u>th</u>umb
☐	☐	☐	☐	☐	☐	☐

G. Recognises the initial grapheme of the word: points to the word that starts with...(*teacher reads choices – refer to soundlist*).

<u>d</u>og	jog	fog	☐
<u>q</u>uit	sit	hit	☐
tall	<u>b</u>all	wall	☐
<u>r</u>ed	ted	fed	☐
met	<u>j</u>et	bet	☐
wig	big	<u>p</u>ig	☐
fat	<u>th</u>at	chat	☐

H. Can write the initial grapheme of words (*child looks at picture and writes grapheme – no help*).

<u>f</u>an	<u>q</u>ueen	<u>b</u>ed	<u>r</u>at	<u>j</u>ug	<u>p</u>in	<u>th</u>umb
☐	☐	☐	☐	☐	☐	☐

Step 4

Teacher Recording Sheet 4.3

I. Can hear the final phoneme of ... (*teacher reads*).

sti**ff** ☐   ja**b** ☐   ho**p** ☐   wi**th** ☐   si**ng** ☐

J. Can say the final phoneme of ... (*child looks at picture on sheet and says sound*).

cli**ff**	bi**b**	ste**p**	pa**th**	ri**ng**
☐	☐	☐	☐	☐

K. Recognises the final grapheme of the word: points to the word that ends with ...(*teacher reads choices – refer to soundlist*).

ti**ff**	till	ting	☐
jot	jo**b**	jog	☐
rat	ra**p**	rag	☐
bask	bash	ba**th**	☐
lo**ng**	lost	logs	☐

L. Can write the final grapheme of words (*child looks at picture and writes grapheme – no help*).

cli**ff**	bi**b**	ta**p**	ba**th**	wi**ng**
☐	☐	☐	☐	☐

M. Score _____ /20 correct

N. Score _____ /20 correct

Steps in Phonics Assessment is published by Hodder & Stoughton Educational. The publishers grant permission for photocopies of this sheet to be made for use solely in the purchasing institution.

Step 4
Picture sheet for Part B

4B

Step 4
Word choice sheet for Part C

4C

pin	pan	pen
jet	jot	jut
sit	set	sat
pup	pip	pop
bud	bed	bid

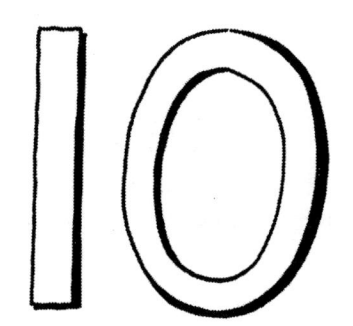

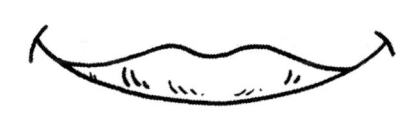

Step 4
Picture sheet for Part D

4D

Step 4
Picture sheet for Part F

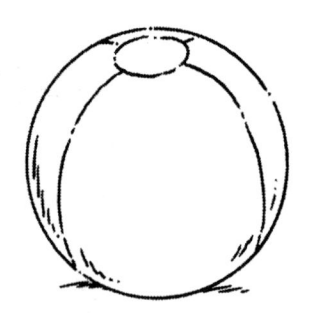

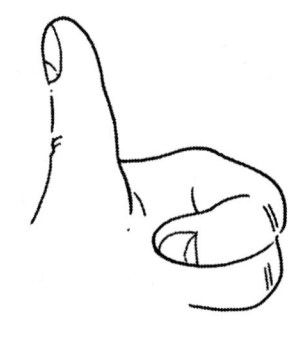

4F

Step 4
Word choice sheet for Part D

4G

dog	jog	fog
quit	sit	hit
tall	ball	wall
red	ted	fed
met	jet	bet
wig	big	pig
fat	that	chat

Steps in Phonics Assessment is published by Hodder & Stoughton Educational. The publishers grant permission for photocopies of this sheet to be made for use solely in the purchasing institution.

Step 4
Picture sheet for Part H

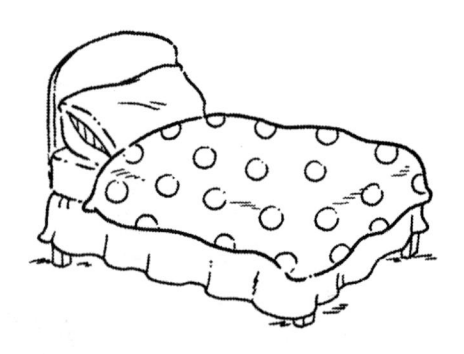

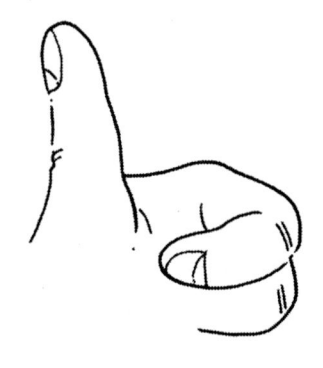

4H

Step 4
Picture sheet for Part J

4J

Step 4
Word choice sheet for Part K

4K

| tiff | till | ting |

| jot | job | jog |

| rat | rap | rag |

| bask | bash | bath |

| long | lost | logs |

Steps in Phonics Assessment is published by Hodder & Stoughton Educational. The publishers grant permission for photocopies of this sheet to be made for use solely in the purchasing institution.

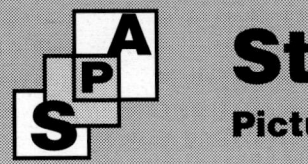

Step 4
Picture sheet for Part L

4L

Step 4

Part M: Spelling C-V-C words

4M

Name_____ Date_____ Assessed by_____

1. I hit the ball with a _____.

2. A boy grows up into a _____.

3. Unkind people make me _____.

4. I like _____ sandwiches.

5. I can hop on one _____.

6. Five and five make _____ .

7. I have a _____ dog .

8. _____ is a bright colour .

9. A _____ keeps a baby clean .

10. I like to _____ races .

11. Please _____ still on the carpet .

12. A _____ is a small seed .

13. We use a _____ to catch fish .

14. I do _____ like creepy-crawlies .

15. I like to _____ to keep fit .

16. Frogs can _____ on lily pads .

17. It is _____ to play games .

18. We use scissors to _____ paper .

19. I _____ a hole with a spade .

20. Pigs like to roll in the _____ .

Step 4

Part N: Spelling C-V-C words

4N

Name_____ Date_____ Assessed by_____

1. I hit the ball with a _____ . (bat bad bet)

2. A boy grows up into a _____ . (mad man men)

3. Unkind people make me _____. (sat cad sad)

4. I like _____ sandwiches. (gum jim jam)

5. I can hop on one _____ . (log leg beg)

6. Five and five make _____. (ten pen hen)

7. I have a _____ dog . (bet pat pet)

8. _____ is a bright colour . (Rub Red Rod)

9. A _____ keeps a baby clean . (bib rib bob)

10. I like to _____ races . (wig pin win)

11. Please _____ still on the carpet . (sat sit wit)

12. A _____ is a small seed . (pig jig pip)

4N cont.

13. We use a _____ to catch fish . (red rod rob)

14. I do _____ like creepy-crawlies . (not hot hop)

15. I like to _____ to keep fit . (jug jig jog)

16. Frogs can _____ on lily pads . (hip hot hop)

17. It is _____ to play games . (fun gun sun)

18. We use scissors to _____ paper . (rut cut cat)

19. I _____ a hole with a spade . (dug dig jug)

20. Pigs like to roll in the _____ . (mad mud mum)

Step 5

Teacher Recording Sheet 5.1

Name_____ Date_____ Assessed by_____

A. Can hear the initial phoneme of ... (*teacher reads*). Can hear the final phoneme of:

<u>v</u>est ☐   <u>w</u>et ☐   <u>y</u>acht ☐   <u>z</u>oo ☐   fo<u>x</u> ☐

B. Can say the initial phoneme of ... (*child looks at picture on sheet and says sound*).

| <u>v</u>an | <u>w</u>heel | <u>y</u>acht | <u>z</u>ip |

And the final phoneme of: bo<u>x</u>

C. Recognises the initial/final grapheme of the word ...: points to the word that has this sound at the start of the word (*teacher reads choices – refer to soundlist*).

<u>v</u>et   met   pet   ☐

jig   <u>w</u>ig   dig   ☐

<u>y</u>et   get   let   ☐

lip   nip   <u>z</u>ip   ☐

Points to the word that ends with this sound:

sip   si<u>x</u>   sit   ☐

D. Can write the initial/final grapheme of the picture words (*child looks at picture and writes grapheme – no help*).

☐ ☐ ☐ ☐ ☐

Step 5

Teacher Recording Sheet 5.2

E. Can hear phonemes within initial consonant clusters (*teacher reads words*).

blood ☐	brown ☐	close ☐	crack ☐
draw ☐	dwell ☐	fly ☐	fridge ☐
glide ☐	grass ☐	please ☐	prize ☐
school ☐	scratch ☐	skip ☐	slide ☐
smile ☐	snack ☐	spend ☐	splash ☐
spread ☐	squash ☐	stone ☐	straight ☐
swan ☐	trick ☐	twist ☐	throw ☐
shrink ☐			

F. Can say the initial consonant cluster (*child looks at picture and says initial phonemes/cluster*).

black	brick	clown	crab	drum	flag
☐	☐	☐	☐	☐	☐

frog	glove	grapes	plug	pram	scarf
☐	☐	☐	☐	☐	☐

screen	skate	sleeve	smoke	snake	spade
☐	☐	☐	☐	☐	☐

square	stamp	swing	tree	twelve	three
☐	☐	☐	☐	☐	☐

Step 5

Teacher Recording Sheet 5.3

G. Can hear phonemes within final consonant clusters *(teacher reads words)*.

ho**ld** ☐   be**nd** ☐   si**lk** ☐   wi**nk** ☐

whi**sk** ☐   he**lp** ☐   ju**mp** ☐   cri**sp** ☐

a**ct** ☐   so**ft** ☐   me**lt** ☐   se**nt** ☐

ke**pt** ☐   te**st** ☐   ne**xt** ☐   e**lf** ☐

lu**nch** ☐   hea**lth** ☐

H. Can say the final consonant cluster *(child looks at picture and says final phonemes/cluster)*.

| go**ld** | ha**nd** | mi**lk** | ta**nk** | di**sk** |

| be**lt** | te**nt** | ne**st** | she**lf** | bra**nch** |

I. Score _____ /25 correct

J. Score _____ /25 correct

K. Score _____ /18 correct

L. Score _____ /18 correct

Steps in Phonics Assessment is published by Hodder & Stoughton Educational. The publishers grant permission for photocopies of this sheet to be made for use solely in the purchasing institution.

Step 5

Picture sheet for Part B

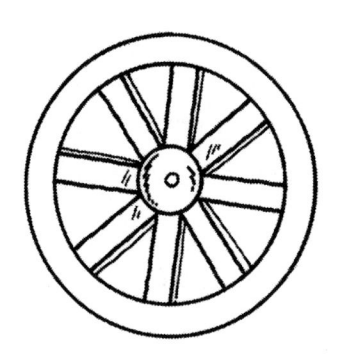

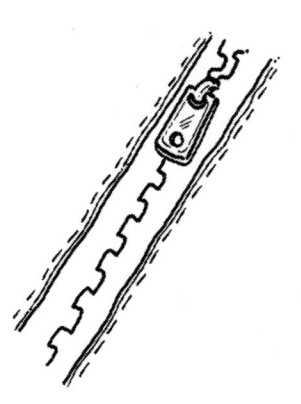

5B

Step 5

Word choice sheet for Part C

5C

vet	met	pet
jig	wig	dig
yet	get	let
lip	nip	zip
sip	six	sit

Step 5
Picture sheet for Part F

5F

Step 5

Picture sheet for Part H

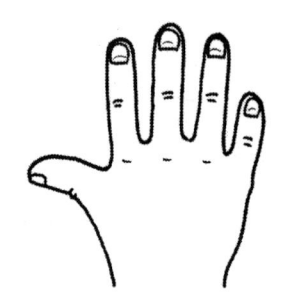

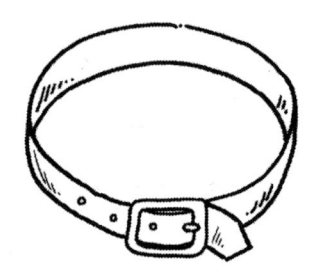

5H

Step 5

Part I: Spelling initial consonant clusters plus vowel consonant

51

Name_____ Date_____ Assessed by_____

1. The darkest colour is _____ .

2. _____s are used to build houses.

3. I can _____ my hands.

4. A _____ walks sideways.

5. We can bang a _____ .

6. A square is a _____ shape.

7. A _____ hops into a pond.

8. I am so _____ you've come to tea.

9. My _____ is an old lady.

10. A _____ is a juicy, purple fruit.

11. A baby rides in a _____ .

12. Put the rubbish on the _____ heap.

13. My _____ is soft and smooth.

14. Don't _____ on the icy road.

15. Don't _____ the window!

16. Scissors can _____ paper.

17. Can you _____ the mistake?

18. I like to _____ in the water.

19. In _____ the birds build their nests.

20. A red light means _____ .

21. We had to _____ the baby in the car seat.

22. I like to _____ in the pool.

23. We went on a school _____ .

24. I wish I had a _____ sister.

25. It is rude to _____ your shoulders.

Steps in Phonics Assessment is published by Hodder & Stoughton Educational. The publishers grant permission for photocopies of this sheet to be made for use solely in the purchasing institution.

Step 5

Part J: Reading initial consonant clusters plus vowel consonant

5J

Name_____ Date_____ Assessed by_____

1. The darkest colour is _____. (black   block   slack)

2. _____s are used to build houses. (Brick   Broke   Trick)

3. I can _____ my hands. (clip   clap   slap)

4. A _____ walks sideways. (grab   crab   cram)

5. We can bang a _____. (drip   drag   drum)

6. A square is a _____ shape. (slat   flag   flat)

7. A _____ hops into a pond. (trog   from   frog)

8. I am so _____ you've come to tea. (glad   glum   flap)

9. My _____ is an old lady. (gran   bran   grab)

10. A _____ is a juicy, purple fruit. (glum   plod   plum)

11. A baby rides in a _____. (prim   pram   tram)

12. Put the rubbish on the _____ heap. (scrap   scrub   strap)

13. My _____ is soft and smooth. (skin   scin   skid)

14. Don't _____ on the icy road. (slip slap clip)

15. Don't _____ the window! (crash smash smack)

16. Scissors can _____ paper. (snip nips pins)

17. Can you _____ the mistake? (slot spin spot)

18. I like to _____ in the water. (splosh splash squash)

19. In _____ the birds build their nests. (Spring Sprint String)

20. A red light means _____ . (tops spot stop)

21. We had to _____ the baby in the car seat. (strap strip scrap)

22. I like to _____ in the pool. (twig swig swim)

23. We went on a school _____ . (drip trip trap)

24. I wish I had a _____ sister. (twig twit twin)

25. It is rude to _____ your shoulders. (shrub shrug scrub)

Steps in Phonics Assessment is published by Hodder & Stoughton Educational. The publishers grant permission for photocopies of this sheet to be made for use solely in the purchasing institution.

Step 5

Part K: Spelling consonant vowel plus consonant clusters

5K

Name_____ Date_____ Assessed by_____

1. _____ on tight to the rail.

2. There is a _____ in the road.

3. _____ comes from cows.

4. _____ is a pretty colour.

5. The old elephant had lost a _____ .

6. _____ me! I'm falling.

7. Ouch! We rode over a _____ .

8. The apple was _____ and juicy.

9. The girl wanted to _____ on the stage.

10. My aunt sent me a birthday _____.

11. The ice-cream began to _____ in the sun.

12. We _____ for a walk.

13. I _____ up the crumbs.

14. I got _____ in the fog.

15. You are _____ in the queue.

16. Can you reach the top _____?

17. I had sandwiches in my packed _____.

18. Can you _____ the ball?

Steps in Phonics Assessment is published by Hodder & Stoughton Educational. The publishers grant permission for photocopies of this sheet to be made for use solely in the purchasing institution.

Step 5

Part L: Reading consonant vowel plus consonant clusters

5L

Name_____ Date_____ Assessed by_____

1. _____ on tight to the rail. (Hold Holt Holk)

2. There is a _____ in the road. (belt bend best)

3. _____ comes from cows. (Mink Mist Milk)

4. _____ is a pretty colour. (Pick Pint Pink)

5. The old elephant had lost a _____. (tusk tunk tunt)

6. _____ me! I'm falling. (Hemp Help Helt)

7. Ouch! We rode over a _____. (bump burp bunk)

8. The apple was _____ and juicy. (crist crisp crisk)

9. The girl wanted to _____ on the stage. (akt ach act)

10. My aunt sent me a birthday _____. (gist gift gilt)

11. The ice-cream began to _____ in the sun. (melt ment mest)

12. We _____ for a walk. (wend welt went)

13. I _____ up the crumbs. (sweep swept swelt)

14. I got _____ in the fog. (losp lont lost)

15. You are _____ in the queue. (nest nelt next)

16. Can you reach the top _____? (shelf shell shelk)

17. I had sandwiches in my packed _____. (lurch lutch lunch)

18. Can you _____ the ball? (catch canch cash)

Steps in Phonics Assessment is published by Hodder & Stoughton Educational. The publishers grant permission for photocopies of this sheet to be made for use solely in the purchasing institution.

Step 6

Part A: Spelling words with common long-vowel digraphs

6A

Name_____ Date_____ Assessed by_____

1. I _____ for my shopping.

2. A ship _____s on the sea.

3. I had a _____ in my leg.

4. Plant the _____ in the ground.

5. There are seven days in a _____ .

6. How do you _____ today?

7. Where have you _____ ?

8. The water is very _____ .

9. Will you _____ me later?

10. I love apple _____ and custard.

11. The little boy _____ his laces.

12. The main _____ had a lot of traffic.

13. The footballer scored a _____.

14. Wash your hands with _____.

15. Put your _____ on, it's cold outside.

16. The builders mended the _____.

17. It is _____ in the shade.

18. The _____ was clean and tidy.

19. The _____ shone brightly at night.

20. The plant had a very long _____.

Step 6

Part B: Reading words with common long-vowel digraphs

6B

Name_____ Date_____ Assessed by_____

1. I _____ for my shopping. (paid pade payd)

2. A ship _____s on the sea. (sale sail sayl)

3. I had a _____ in my leg. (pain pane payn)

4. Plant the _____ in the ground. (sede sead seed)

5. There are seven days in a _____ . (weak weke week)

6. How do you _____ today? (feal feel fele)

7. Where have you _____ ? (been bean bene)

8. The water is very _____ . (deap depe deep)

9. Will you _____ me later? (meet meat mete)

10. I love apple _____ and custard. (py pie piy)

11. The little boy _____ his laces. (tied tide tyde)

12. The main _____ had a lot of traffic. (rood rode road)

13. The footballer scored a _____ . (goal gowl gole)

6B cont.

14. Wash your hands with _____ . (soap sowp sope)

15. Put your _____ on, it's cold outside. (cote coat cowt)

16. The builders mended the _____ . (rufe rouf roof)

17. It is _____ in the shade. (cule cewl cool)

18. The _____ was clean and tidy. (rume room rewm)

19. The _____ shone brightly at night. (mewn moon mune)

20. The plant had a very long _____ . (rewt rute root)

Steps in Phonics Assessment is published by Hodder & Stoughton Educational. The publishers grant permission for photocopies of this sheet to be made for use solely in the purchasing institution.

Step 6

Part C: Spelling words with more common vowel digraphs

6C

Name_____ Date_____ Assessed by_____

1. Some people use a knife and _____ to eat.

2. The baby was _____ in the hospital.

3. Could you please _____ it out?

4. The children all worked very _____ .

5. The family went for a walk in the _____ .

6. "Old MacDonald had a _____ ."

7. The owl flew into the _____ .

8. _____ scissors cut better.

9. A wheel is _____ of a car.

10. The _____ made a nest.

11. My sister is a little _____ .

12. Your shoes are covered in _____ !

13. A kettle will _____ water.

14. I'd like to _____ the recorder club.

15. Please don't _____ at me.

Steps in Phonics Assessment is published by Hodder & Stoughton Educational. The publishers grant permission for photocopies of this sheet to be made for use solely in the purchasing institution.

Step 6

Part D: Reading words with more common vowel digraphs

6D

Name_____ Date_____ Assessed by_____

1. Some people use a knife and _____ to eat. (fork fark fouk)

2. The baby was _____ in the hospital. (boon born barn)

3. Could you please _____ it out? (sort soot sart)

4. The children all worked very _____. (haid herd hard)

5. The family went for a walk in the _____. (park pork paik)

6. "Old MacDonald had a _____." (firm farm fame)

7. The owl flew into the _____. (bain born barn)

8. _____ scissors cut better. (Shape Sharp Shorp)

9. A wheel is _____ of a car. (pait port part)

10. The _____ made a nest. (bird bard bind)

11. My sister is a little _____. (goil girl garl)

12. Your shoes are covered in _____! (dint dart dirt)

13. A kettle will _____ water. (boil borl bail)

14. I'd like to _____ the recorder club. (jain join jorn)

15. Please don't _____ at me. (shunt short shout)

Steps in Phonics Assessment is published by Hodder & Stoughton Educational. The publishers grant permission for photocopies of this sheet to be made for use solely in the purchasing institution.

Step 7

Part A: Spelling words containing more long vowel digraphs and trigraphs

7A

Name_____ Date_____ Assessed by_____

1. Pardon, what did you _____ ?

2. Is this the right _____ ?

3. I _____ a model.

4. The bird was kept in a _____ .

5. The birthday _____ had six candles.

6. This house is for _____ .

7. What is your _____ ?

8. A circle is a round _____ .

9. Close the _____ behind you.

10. I _____ up my pocket money.

11. I like to _____ books.

12. A _____ is part of a plant .

13. It's your turn to _____ the cards.

14. I was picked to play in the football _____ .

15. Sorry, I didn't _____ it.

16. Things are _____ if they don't cost much money.

17. The fire gave out a lot of _____ .

18. At midday the sun is _____ in the sky.

19. It's dark, switch on the _____.

20. I am kind and share _____ toys.

21. "Three blind _____" is a well-known rhyme.

22. I can _____ a bike.

23. In Spring the trees seem to come to _____.

24. I _____ to have fun.

25. Put your books in a tidy _____.

26. Is it nearly dinner _____?

27. Give that back, it's _____!

28. _____ your dirty feet!

29. Can you _____ into the pool?

30. I _____ my bike down the hill.

31. That is a funny _____.

32. Don't fall down the _____!

33. I want to go _____!

34. The dog chews the _____.

35. I _____ I get this right!

36. A _____ is a lovely scented flower.

37. Who will you _____ for?

38. Someone stood on my _____.

39. The seeds _____ into plants.

40. The sky looks _____ on a sunny day.

41. It is _____ to stare.

42. An elephant is a _____ animal.

43. I can play a _____ on the piano.

44. An electric plug has a _____.

45. The little baby looked very _____.

Step 7

Part B: Reading words containing more long-vowel digraphs and trigraphs

7B

Name_____ Date_____ Assessed by_____

1. Pardon, what did you _____? (say sai sae)

2. Is this the right _____ ? (plais place plays)

3. I _____ a model. (maid made mayd)

4. The bird was kept in a _____. (caij cayj cage)

5. The birthday _____ had six candles. (caik cayk cake)

6. This house is for _____. (sale sail sayl)

7. What is your _____? (name naim naym)

8. A circle is a round _____. (shape shayp shaip)

9. Close the _____ behind you. (gait gate gayt)

10. I _____ up my pocket money. (saiv sayv save)

11. I like to _____ books. (read rede reed)

12. A _____ is part of a plant. (leaf leef lefe)

13. It's your turn to _____ the cards. (deel dele deal)

14. I was picked to play in the football _____. (teem teme team)

15. Sorry, I didn't _____ it. (mean meen mene)

16. Things are _____ if they don't cost much money. (cheep chepe cheap)

17. The fire gave out a lot of _____. (heet hete heat)

7B cont.

18. At midday the sun is _____ in the sky. (high hie hy)

19. It's dark, switch on the _____. (lite light liet)

20. I am kind and share _____ toys. (my mi mie)

21. "Three blind _____" is a well-known rhyme.(mies mice myce)

22. I can _____ a bike. (ride ryde ried)

23. In Spring the trees seem to come to _____. (lyf lief life)

24. I _____ to have fun. (like like lyke)

25. Put your books in a tidy _____. (pile pyle piel)

26. Is it nearly dinner _____? (tyme time tiem)

27. Give that back, it's _____! (mine myne mien)

28. _____ your dirty feet! (Wipe Wiep Wype)

29. Can you _____ into the pool? (dyve diev dive)

30. I _____ my bike down the hill. (rode road rowd)

31. That is a funny _____. (joak joke jowk)

32. Don't fall down the _____! (hole howl hoal)

33. I want to go _____! (hoam hoem home)

34. The dog chews the _____. (boan boen bone)

7B cont.

35. I _____ I get this right! (hope hoap hoep)

36. A _____ is a lovely scented flower. (rows rose roas)

37. Who will you _____ for? (voet voat vote)

38. Someone stood on my _____. (toe tow toa)

39. The seeds _____ into plants. (grew grue groo)

40. The sky looks _____ on a sunny day. (bloo blew blue)

41. It is _____ to stare. (rood rude rewd)

42. An elephant is a _____ animal. (huge hewg hooj)

43. I can play a _____ on the piano. (tune toon tewn)

44. An electric plug has a _____. (fews foos fuse)

45. The little baby looked very _____. (coot cute cuet)

Step 7

Part C: Spelling words containing more vowel digraphs and trigraphs

7C

Name_____ Date_____ Assessed by_____

1. A _____ grows up into a man.

2. The dog began to _____ .

3. A _____ has many shops.

4. How high can you _____ a ball?

5. The seeds had _____ into plants.

6. A group of cattle is called a _____ .

7. We have a holiday at half- _____ .

8. The baby's hair began to _____ .

9. Ouch! I _____ myself.

10. A _____ is a bird of prey.

11. The baby learns to _____ .

12. Please sit on the _____ .

13. Pardon, I didn't _____ you.

14. The children were very _____ .

15. The _____ is very interesting to read.

Steps in Phonics Assessment is published by Hodder & Stoughton Educational. The publishers grant permission for photocopies of this sheet to be made for use solely in the purchasing institution.

Step 7

Part D: Can spell words containing more vowel digraphs and trigraphs

7D

Name_____ Date_____ Assessed by_____

1. A _____ grows up into a man. (boi boy bow)

2. The dog began to _____. (howl houl hole)

3. A _____ has many shops. (toun town tone)

4. How high can you _____ a ball? (throw throe threw)

5. The seeds had _____ into plants. (grone grown groan)

6. A group of cattle is called a _____. (hird hurd herd)

7. We have a holiday at half-_____. (term tirm turm)

8. The baby's hair began to _____. (curl cirl cerl)

9. Ouch! I _____ myself. (hert hirt hurt)

10. A _____ is a bird of prey. (hork hawk hark)

11. The baby learns to _____. (crawl crorl crarl)

12. Please sit on the _____. (chear chare chair)

13. Pardon, I didn't _____ you. (hear here heer)

14. The children were very _____. (goud gud good)

15. The _____ is very interesting to read. (bouk book buck)

Steps in Phonics Assessment is published by Hodder & Stoughton Educational. The publishers grant permission for photocopies of this sheet to be made for use solely in the purchasing institution.

Steps in Phonics Assessment — Class Record Sheet

Year : Teacher :		Assessments				
Child's name	Start date	Date	Date	Date	Target	Finish date

Steps in Phonics Assessment is published by Hodder & Stoughton Educational. The publishers grant permission for photocopies of this sheet to be made for use solely in the purchasing institution.

SPA Individual Record Sheet

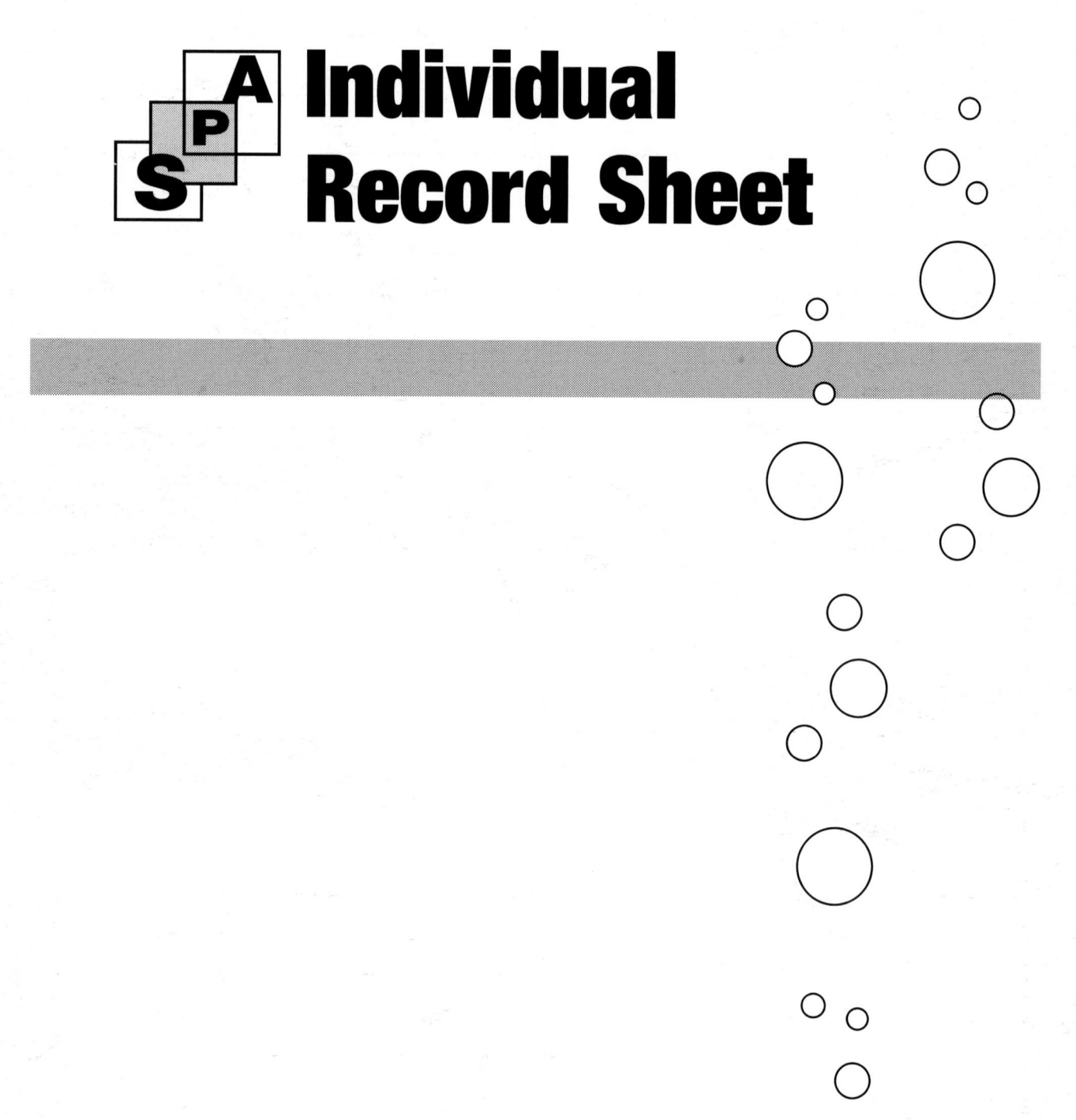

This Individual Record Sheet is not photocopiable: copies are available separately to enable you to maintain a cumulative record and to track each pupil's progress from Step 1 through to mastery of Step 7.

(pack of 20 copies ISBN 0 340 79948 X)

Steps in Phonics Assessment

Individual Record Sheet

Pupil's name _____
Date of birth _____
Nursery / Pre-school   Yes / No
Special Needs   Yes / No
English as an Additional Language   Yes / No

SPECIMEN

School _____
Date of entry _____

ASSESSMENT ON ENTRY	Assessed by	Date	Step

END-OF-YEAR ASSESSMENT SUMMARY

Year R	Assessed by	Date	Step
Year 1	Assessed by	Date	Step
Year 2	Assessed by	Date	Step
Year 3	Assessed by	Date	Step
Year 4	Assessed by	Date	Step

STEP 1		score	% score	date	Action
	Sound discrimination				

STEP 2		score	% score	date	Action
A	Rhymes				
	Initial phonemes: s, m, c/k, t, g, h				
B	- can hear				
C	- can say				
	Initial graphemes: s, m, c/k, t, g, h				
D	- can read				
E	- can write				

STEP 3		score	% score	date	Action
	Final phonemes: s, m, c/k, t, g				
A	- can hear				
B	- can say				
	Final graphemes: s(ss), m, ck, t, g				
C	- can read				
D	- can write				
	Initial phonemes: l, n, d, sh, ch				
E	- can hear				
F	- can say				
	Initial graphemes: l, n, d, sh, ch				
G	- can read				
H	- can write				
	Final phonemes: l(ll), n, d, sh, ch				
I	- can hear				
J	- can say				
	Final graphemes: l, n, d, sh, ch				
K	- can read				
L	- can write				

STEP 4		score	% score	date	Action
	Medial vowel phonemes: a, e, i, o, u				
A	- can hear				
B	- can say				
	Medial vowel graphemes: a, e, i, o, u				
C	- can read				
D	- can write				
	Initial phonemes: f, qu, b, r, j, p, th				
E	- can hear				
F	- can say				
	Initial graphemes: f, qu, b, r, j, p, th				
G	- can read				
H	- can write				
	Final phonemes: f(ff), b, p, th, ng				
I	- can hear				
J	- can say				
	Final graphemes: f(ff), b, p, th, ng				
K	- can read				
L	- can write				
M	Can spell C-V-C words				
N	Can read C-V-C words				

STEP 5		score	% score	date	Action
	Initial/final phonemes: v, w, x, y, z				
A	- can hear				
B	- can say				
	Initial/final graphemes: v, w, x, y, z				
C	- can read				
D	- can write				
	Initial consonant clusters				
E	- can hear				
F	- can say				
	Final consonant clusters				
G	- can hear				
H	- can say				
I	Can spell CC-V-C words				
J	Can read CC-V-C words				
K	Can spell C-V-CC words				
L	Can read C-V-CC words				

	STEP 6	score	% score	date	Action
A	Can spell words with common long-vowel digraphs: ai, ee, ie, oa, oo				
B	Can read words with common long-vowel digraphs: ai, ee, ie, oa, oo				
C	Can spell words with common vowel digraphs: or, ar, ir, oi, ou				
D	Can read words with common vowel digraphs: or, ar, ir, oi, ou				

	STEP 7	score	% score	date	Action
A	Can spell words with more long-vowel digraphs & trigraphs: ay, a-e, ea, igh, y, i-e, o-e, oe, ew, ue, u-e				
B	Can read words with more long-vowel digraphs & trigraphs: ay, a-e, ea, igh, y, i-e, o-e, oe, ew, ue, u-e				
C	Can spell words with more vowel digraphs & trigraphs: oy, ow(ou), ow(oa), er, ur, aw, air, ear, oo(look)				
D	Can read words with more vowel digraphs & trigraphs: oy, ow(ou), ow(oa), er, ur, aw, air, ear, oo(look)				

ISBN 0 340 79948 X (*pack of 20 copies*) Impression number 10 9 8 7 6 5 4 3 2 1
Copyright © 2000 Deborah Oldham Year 2005 2004 2003 2002 2001 2000
All rights reserved. No part of this publication may be reproduced or transmitted in any form or by any means, electronic or mechanical, including photocopy, recording or any information storage and retrieval system, without permission in writing from the publisher.

This publication is excluded from the reprographic licensing scheme administered by the Copyright Licensing Agency Ltd.
The published edition of this record sheet is printed in a coloured ink: please contact the publisher if your copy is printed in black.
Printed in Great Britain for Hodder & Stoughton Educational, the educational publishing division of Hodder Headline Plc, 338 Euston Road, London NW1 3BH, by Hobbs The Printers, Totton, Hants.